About the Book

Joseph M. Dukert takes a complete and authoritative look at the nuclear-powered ships of the world, military and commercial. More than 200 ships fly the flags of six different countries. They range from the mightiest warship to a peaceful ore hauler.

Mr. Dukert reports on how nuclear ships and submarines work. He describes the first ships launched, surveys today's fleet, and projects the future. The advantages and disadvantages of building and maintaining a nuclear fleet are discussed along with pros and cons that have been voiced. He attempts to answer important questions: How safe are nuclear ships? Why nuclear propulsion? How do Russian subs compare to ours? Can commercial nuclear ships succeed? Are they practical? And can they make a profit?

Accurate and interesting information is given on reactors, hulls, and propulsion along with a fascinating description of what it means to live aboard a nuclear-powered sub which virtually becomes a self-contained "town" underwater, complete with the necessities and some of the luxuries—piped-in music, daily movies, a ship's library, gymnasium equipment.

Striking black-and-white photographs give a dramatic picture of the nuclear ships of the world.

UNITED STATES

GREAT BRITAIN

FRANCE

GERMANY

USSR

NUCLEAR SHIPS OF THE WORLD

by Joseph M. Dukert

Coward, McCann & Geoghegan, Inc.
New York

THIS BOOK IS FOR BETTY

Second Impression

Copyright © 1973 by Joseph M. Dukert

SBN: GB: 698-30501-9
SBN: TR: 698-20248-1
Library of Congress Catalog Card Number: 72-89765

PRINTED IN THE UNITED STATES OF AMERICA

Photo Credits

Contents

A U.S. Navy Skyhawk comes in for a landing on the atomic-powered aircraft carrier Enterprise. *Beyond are the frigate* Bainbridge *and the cruiser* Long Beach, *both nuclear powered.*

The First Two Hundred Were Just the Beginning

There are more nuclear power plants operating at sea right now than on land. More than two hundred nuclear-powered ships have been built so far. They fly the flags of half a dozen countries: the United States, the Soviet Union, the United Kingdom, France, the Federal Republic of Germany, and Japan. It won't be long before other countries—including the People's Republic of China—join this group.

Already, nuclear propulsion has changed every country's ideas about war and defense. In time, peaceful atomic vessels will help make equally great changes in travel and commerce.

By the 1980's, the world's nuclear fleet will probably be twice as large as it was in 1970. Before the end of the twentieth century, its makeup may change too. Nuclear-driven commercial ships should finally begin to outnumber atomic ships of war.

There will be totally new types. Peaceful nuclear vessels will speed comfortably across the seas—and under their surface too. By the year 2000 they should help to establish "farms" and "mines" in the oceans' depths. Some atomic merchantmen may carry tourists from New York to Western Europe in a single day.

These are fairly safe predictions to make, because we know a lot more about nuclear ship propulsion than most people realize. It is no longer really *new*.

The first vessel to be powered by a nuclear reactor was the U.S. submarine *Nautilus*. Like the submarine of the same name in Jules Verne's fictional story, *Twenty Thousand Leagues Under the Sea*, the new *Nautilus* thrilled people who read about it and excited their imagination. Its power and endurance were remarkable; its success in 1958 in reaching the ice-covered North Pole was dramatic. Compared to today's atomic submarines, however (and in spite of periodic overhauls to "modernize" the ship), *Nautilus* is old-fashioned.

Nautilus began its service a long time ago—1954; and even some subs which came later are outmoded now in one way or another. *Triton*, for instance, was publicized widely in the early 1960's. Powered by two reactors instead of one, it was the longest submarine ever built. On its very first cruise, *Triton*'s secret assignment was to impress the world during a period of international tension by showing how small our planet had become. It succeeded; *Triton* was the first vessel to circle the earth completely without surfacing. That was a fantastic achievement at the time, yet less than ten years later *Triton* was "put into mothballs" at Portsmouth, Virginia. Its twin reactors were shut down, and their fuel cores were taken out so that the fissionable material in them could be reused. All equipment that could be pulled out easily was removed; and *Triton*'s hull was covered with protective gunk—in case some new use was found later for this first "relic" of the Nuclear Shipping Age.

Admiral Hyman G. Rickover, "the father of the nuclear navy," expected such developments. Admiral Rickover has earned the reputation of being a restless, quick-tempered, sarcastic man; but his engineering bril-

The N.S. Savannah, *greeted here on its arrival in New York Harbor, was the first nuclear merchant ship.*

liance and persistence enabled him to accomplish more than anybody else in the world in translating theories about nuclear ships into real equipment that worked. In 1957, while there were still only *two* nuclear ships in the world instead of *two hundred,* the fiery and farsighted admiral insisted:

> . . . *Nautilus* did not mark the end of a technological road. It marked the beginning. It should be compared with the first airplane that flew at Kitty Hawk. It marks the beginning of a technological revolution at sea.

That's also true of the first nuclear merchant ship. The American-built *Savannah* was never intended to operate profitably; it toured the globe for about eight years as a sort of seagoing exhibit. It visited more than seventy-five ports, and millions of people saw it. Engineers learned

The North Pole has become a meeting place for nuclear sub-marines. (Top photo), U.S.S. Seadragon and Skate sit nose to nose after breaking through the ice at the top of the world. (Middle), the British sub Dreadnought punches through polar ice on a winter visit. (Below), the Russians' Leninsky Komsomol.

from it. This first nuclear merchant ship helped to set new kinds of safety standards, and it gave crews and shipping companies an idea of what it might be like to operate commercial nuclear fleets in the future.

Savannah did its job well, but it was retired in 1970 to become a floating museum. To compare *Savannah* (or even a much newer ship, like Germany's ore-hauling *Otto Hahn*) with the nuclear cargo ships being designed in many countries now is like comparing the first astronaut's orbit of the earth with the moon landings of Apollo—or even with the launching of a space laboratory. Basic principles stay the same, but they are used in different ways, on a different scale, with very different goals.

Many people predicted years ago that commercial atomic shipping would develop more quickly than it has. Most of them made this mistake because they didn't stop to analyze either the advantages or the disadvantages of ocean propulsion by atomic energy. Furthermore, many newspaper and magazine articles have given the impression that all nuclear ships are pretty much alike. Of course, they *aren't*, and one aim of this book is to explain in simple terms *why* they aren't.

To do that, it's necessary to look at how nuclear energy is actually harnessed when "the atom goes to sea." Safety and costs are important as well, so they must both be considered too. There are also limits to what either manufacturers or their materials can do.

It's easy for an artist to paint attractive pictures of "nuclear ships of the future." Well-trained engineers can produce reasonable-looking drawings of the ships' insides. But *building* them to operate as planned is still a challenge. Once we realize all this, it's easier to appreciate what's going on in the world of nuclear ships. As we look ahead, the problems and prospects become clearer. And the future *does* look bright!

Otto Hahn *brings ore to Hamburg from ports around the world. The Federal Republic of Germany and Japan are cooperating to develop nuclear ships with eight times the power of this one.*

All but a handful of the "nukes" built so far have been warships, and almost all of those have been submarines. The reasons are obvious; atomic subs do things that once were considered impossible:

They can travel all around the world almost invisibly —for months at a time—without stopping or even breaking the surface to take a fresh breath. With two-thirds of the earth's surface as a hiding place, they can fire rocket weapons to reach any enemy metropolis or military base. An atomic sub of any nationality can take shortcuts under the Arctic ice sheet, too, shortening trips by thousands of miles. A single load of nuclear fuel in one of the new ones can drive it almost as far on its voyages as the distance from here to the moon and back. Its speed may be up to 40 knots*—which is really zipping through the water.

Nuclear submarines are not all alike, even though they look that way at a quick glance. Different Navy submarines may have quite different jobs, just as surface ships do. Some subs patrol the seas chiefly as listening

---

* Ship speeds will be listed throughout this book in the traditional naval measurement of "knots." A knot equals 1.15 "land miles" per hour, so a 40-knot speed is the same as 46 miles (or about 73 kilometers) per hour.

posts, but others are underwater bases for ICBM's. The kind that's potentially best for tracking down enemy ships may not be as good for other duties. Sometimes *speed* is essential, while in other cases it's more important to move as *quietly* as possible.

Submarines aren't always weapons of war either. Cargo-carrying nuclear submarines were first suggested many years ago; and much important research in geology, oceanography, zoology, and even glaciology can be carried on only by atomic-powered submersibles. We will need them before long to harvest the sea, as well as to make sure that the earth's oceans do not die. To handle a variety of tasks, it's best to create a variety of designs.

Differences among nuclear-powered surface warships are generally more obvious than those among Navy subs. For example, the U.S. guided-missile frigate *Bainbridge*

Lenin, *the world's first atomic icebreaker, was launched in 1957 and entered service officially two years later.*

S.S. Sealand Galloway, *the world's largest and fastest container ship, is fueled by oil. By 1980 it may be more profitable to operate a ship like this on nuclear power, on certain routes.*

is only slightly bigger and heavier than a modern atomic submarine. That's pretty big—longer than a football field; but it isn't enormous. On the other hand, the mighty *Enterprise* is the largest naval vessel ever built. *Enterprise* was the first of the United States' nuclear aircraft carriers, and if it were tilted up on end it would match the size of some of New York's tallest skyscrapers.

Statistics about size may be fascinating, but they have little to do with the unique values of nuclear propulsion in a surface warship. Speed isn't the only factor either. Nor is the fact that the reactors aboard the newest nuclear ships will need no more than one fresh loading of uranium fuel during a ship's whole lifetime. There are *other* advantages—and there have to be—just to justify the cost.

Nuclear propulsion is expensive at the beginning, even though it may save money in the long run. A country can

18

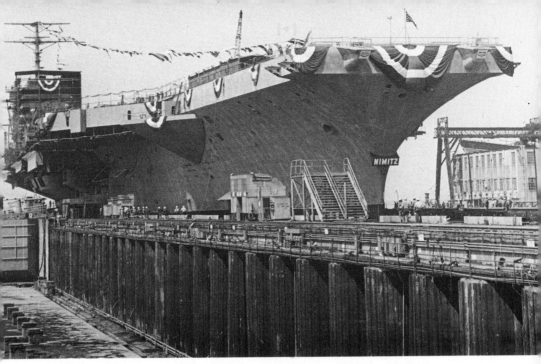

The two nuclear reactors on Nimitz *(above)* are powerful enough to satisfy the electrical needs of a city the size of Syracuse, New York. Nimitz *and sister ship* Eisenhower *(below) will use them to cruise continuously, refueling only once in about twenty-five years.*

add three oil-fueled surface ships to its navy for about the same price as two nuclear ships of the same general type. But nuclear naval ships are favored for several reasons besides the most obvious ones. A nuclear aircraft carrier can handle emergency missions which no oil-burning ship could ever perform.

Peaceful atomic vessels must be considered separately from warships. It isn't generally necessary for commercial ships to be able to outperform their rivals. Most owners and operators aren't willing to pay a lot extra, just so they can boast that their ships are the fastest, or the biggest, or even the most modern. The shipping business is like others; a company must aim first at earning more money than it spends. That's why shipbuilders and line owners in the United States (where costs are relatively high) demand a thorough answer to the question asked by Chapter Eight—"Can Atomic Ships Make a Profit?"

Frankly, the answer to this important question has changed within the past few years. It is still not a simple "Yes" or "No." *Some* nuclear-powered merchant ships will be operating profitably within the next several years; but they will have to be of a certain minimum size, operating in a certain way. To understand *why* this is so (as well as to understand the world's growing atomic war fleets), the best way to begin is by considering *how* nuclear energy propels a ship.

CHAPTER TWO

How Do They Work?

This chapter *might* have been cut down to a single paragraph, instead of being the most complicated part of the book. It would be accurate to say it all in about one hundred words:

Heat from a nuclear reactor turns water into steam. That steam spins turbine blades, the way wind operates a windmill. Then the steam recondenses to water, which goes back to the reactor to be heated again. A rotating turbine can generate electricity for lights and other equipment aboard the ship, so part of the resulting energy is used that way. However, most of the spinning motion within the turbines is used more directly. A set of gears slow it down and increase its force, linking it eventually to an ordinary propeller. As the prop churns through the water, it drives the ship along.

That's all true, as far as it goes. It's the way almost every nuclear ship afloat today works. But that brief description can't explain the great differences in cost between military and civilian nuclear ships. It ignores some interesting experiments in the past and some possibly

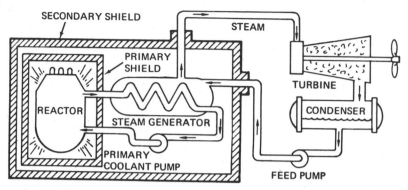

SECONDARY SHIELD
STEAM
PRIMARY SHIELD
TURBINE
REACTOR
STEAM GENERATOR
CONDENSER
PRIMARY COOLANT PUMP
FEED PUMP

A simplified diagram of the major parts of a nuclear ship.

important changes in the future. To understand atomic vessels of all kinds—with both their advantages and their problems—it's better to start with a few fundamental facts about nuclear energy itself.

Theoretically, three distinct kinds of nuclear energy *might* be used to propel ships: (1) nuclear fission; (2) nuclear fusion; and (3) the spontaneous decay of radioactive materials. All three produce heat. The second and third nuclear techniques aren't yet practical for ship propulsion, however. That still leaves a lot to be explained about *nuclear fission*—and how nuclear reactors operate.

Boilers on conventional (*i.e., non*nuclear) ships produce steam, too, but they get their heat from *chemical* reactions (*e.g.,* burning coal or oil). Those chemical reactions involve only the tiny particles at the outer edges of atoms—the *electrons*, which are usually pictured as whirling around each atomic nucleus like planets around the sun. In contrast, *nuclear* reactions involve the heart of the atom itself (its nucleus), where most of the mass is concentrated. When a nucleus splits into pieces, obviously, more matter gets into the act than could possibly be the case in any chemical process.* The heat-energy

---

* In fact, a small part of the mass is converted *completely* into energy during fission, according to Einstein's famous equation, $E = MC^2$. Just imagine what that means in terms of "pushing power," for a ship or anything else:

22

released by a single fissioning atom is roughly a million times what is produced by an atom of conventional fuel like coal or wood or oil or gas when it burns.

Nevertheless, it's misleading to make a statement like: "*Savannah* used only ten pounds of uranium-235 fuel to travel around the world." And it's downright untrue to say (as people often do) that such-and-such nuclear submarine traveled so many thousands of miles on "a grapefruit-sized chunk of uranium." This makes a shipboard reactor sound too much like an ordinary ship boiler—which it *isn't*. When an atomic ship starts to run out of steam, you might suppose that its crew could simply toss a fresh piece of uranium into a nuclear furnace. If today's reactors worked *that* simply, there surely would be two *thousand* ships in the world's nuclear fleet by now instead of slightly more than *two hundred*. Unfortunately, the full story is more complex.

Nuclear energy *can* propel ships more cheaply than oil. But a comparison of the two depends on more than just the price of raw uranium. Plain uranium is not outlandishly expensive. It costs about as much as the chromium which decorates most automobiles. Yet by the time a few hundred pounds of uranium wind up in the core of a modern nuclear submarine that single fuel load costs about $3,500,000. Here's why:

Most ship reactor fuel is produced and loaded in "bundles," such as the one pictured on page 24. The design of the bundles is fairly complex, and each part must be made to precise specifications. This is because, in a way, the *fuel* of a nuclear reactor *is* the reactor. To work prop-

---

The breathtaking factor is "C" (the velocity of light), because light takes only a second to move roughly 186,000 miles—nearly the distance from here to the moon. Yet the energy released (E) is as much as would be involved in sending the same mass of material (M) hurtling through space *at the speed of light* . . . and then somehow multiplying its "energy of motion" by the speed of light *again*.

23

This fresh fuel bundle, shown being inserted into Savannah's reactor, looked much the same several years later, when it was removed after helping to drive the ship for hundreds of thousands of miles. Fissionable uranium was part of a ceramic compound in thousands of pellets, sealed inside the long vertical tubes.

erly, the fueled section of a reactor (called the core) must usually be able to keep its original shape for years— despite very high temperatures and all sorts of stresses.* It can't just burn up, the way most fuels do.

It's true that fissionable atoms are gradually replaced by fission fragments (smaller atoms) as a reactor oper-

* While a typical, modern, commercial shipboard reactor is operating at full power, the temperature on the outer surface of its metal fuel tubes may be only about 315° C. (600° F.). At the center of a fuel pellet inside the tube, however, it's probably close to 1000° C.

ates; but this happens rather evenly in all parts of the core at once. It takes a microscope to see the change in any one spot. In fact, only a small percentage of the original uranium atoms normally disappear in this way before the fuel elements are removed for other reasons. The few "ashes" left behind stay locked inside the fuel elements—amid the unused fuel material, which can be recovered and reused. Because the bundles are then highly radioactive, it's a costly job. Reprocessing should be counted as part of the fuel expense.

One reason why fissionable fuel in a reactor must be positioned so carefully is the very factor that makes nuclear fission a practical energy source: Fission is a process (like fire) which can spread from one "burnable" atom to the others around it. Also like fire, it can be handled safely, but only if you go about it in the right way.

Without going into the details of nuclear physics, it's

A fission chain reaction.

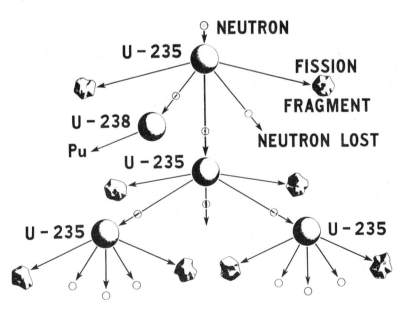

enough to realize that when atomic nuclei split they tend to squirt out *neutrons*. These particles may act like bullets to crack open the nuclei of other fissionable atoms nearby. A successful nuclear fire of this type—one that keeps going by itself—is known as a chain reaction. Each fission is *linked* to the next one.

A chain reaction will continue only if all conditions are right and if the proper sort of atoms are clustered so as to encourage collisions between their nuclei and the neutrons whizzing around them. Fuel elements for a reactor must be designed so that the exact geometry of the core can be known at all times—and changed when necessary to regulate the pace of the reaction.

A reactor never brings all of its fissionable atoms together in a big lump. That's done only in setting off nuclear explosives, where the sudden jamming together of pure fissionable material is exactly what causes the instantaneous heat of a fission explosion. Instead, reactors s-p-a-c-e o-u-t the fissionable atoms within their fuel elements. Reactors are built so that it would be impossible to produce a nuclear explosion inside one even if somebody tried. There's simply no way of bringing enough fissionable material so close together rapidly enough. Instead, the chain reaction in a reactor is controlled. Heat is given off gradually.

A reactor balances its supply of neutron "bullets" and fissionable "targets" carefully, and then the unchanging laws of nature take over. The amount and rate of heat produced is predictable. Different kinds of reactors regulate their neutron supplies in various ways, but usually they start by spreading fissionable atoms evenly throughout a chemical compound. This fuel compound must be able to stand the stress of a reactor's operating environment without melting or crumbling; but it can take different physical shapes. It may be in pellets, plates, rods,

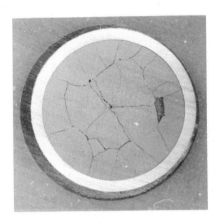

Except for some cracks, a fuel pellet which has been used in a nuclear reactor shows little evidence that billions of its uranium atoms have fissioned to release heat energy. Much of the fuel is intact (although it is mixed now with fission products), and it can be manufactured into new pellets after reprocessing.

slender pins, or hollow cylinders. The fuel-form *could* even be a liquid—either molten metal, a melted uranium salt, or some uranium compound dissolved in water. In any case, however, it's important to remember that some sort of strong cladding (like the metal tubes in the photo on page 24) almost always separates the fissionable material itself from the reactor *coolant*.

The *coolant* is a liquid or a gas which passes through an operating core to take heat away from the fuel elements. This keeps the core from getting *too* hot, and it also delivers the heat energy—as fast as it is produced—to a point where it can be put to work. On a ship, that generally means passing it through a heat exchanger to produce steam.

Besides *fuel* and *coolant*, the other parts of any reactor design which ought to be kept in mind when thinking about shipboard uses are the *moderator* and the *control elements*:

The *moderator* may be either a liquid or a solid. Its

27

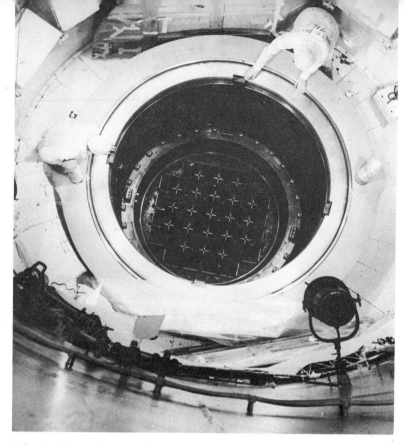

The position of cross-shaped control rods in a ship reactor core shows clearly as technicians prepare to practice loading with dummy fuel bundles.

job is to slow down fast-moving neutrons without stopping them. In most cases, slower-moving neutrons are more efficient in producing fissions within a reactor's fuel.

The *control elements* (normally solid components) contain "nuclear poisons." These are materials that tend to absorb neutrons completely, preventing them from producing new fissions. Control rods can be moved in and out among the fuel elements to change the rate at which a reactor generates power, or to shut it off completely.

Materials used in building a core must be chosen carefully, and they aren't always convenient to work with. For example, the men who planned the *Nautilus* knew almost from the start that the metal zirconium and some of its alloys could make marvelous fuel cladding. An alloy of zirconium and uranium could even be used as the basic fuel material itself. Zirconium doesn't waste many neutrons by absorbing them, and it isn't affected much by either high temperatures or radiation. But at the beginning of the nuclear ship program nobody had ever refined more than a small bit of zirconium. Zirconium ore usually contains another element, *hafnium*—which absorbs neutrons so readily it can be used as a nuclear poison in control rods. Obviously, impurities like that had to be removed completely; but the cost of producing suitably pure zirconium was estimated originally at hundreds of dollars per kilogram. With Admiral Rickover's prodding, however, a mass production system was devised; the price plummeted as ship reactors began to use thousands of tons a year. Nuclear fuel manufacturers learned to weld and work with this once exotic metal, and today nuclear engineers around the world discuss zirconium almost as casually as they speak of stainless steel. Still, there was a long gap between understanding how to design a nuclear ship reactor and being able to *build* one.

A ship's reactor must be able to respond instantly and accurately to the captain's orders. It has to operate reliably and continuously, even while the ship is being tossed about at unpredictable angles by waves. The fuel core itself is like a fine piece of machinery; it depends on delicately engineered spacing to adjust the coolant, moderator, and control elements. A bad scratch on the surface of a single fuel tube might cause problems, because uneven cooling could produce a damaging "hot spot."

Finally, there is one more important detail of reactor design which affects both its cost and the way it performs. It is called *fuel enrichment*.

29

Not all uranium atoms are alike. Less than one in one hundred of those found in nature is the kind known as uranium-235*—the type which fissions most readily in most reactors. The rest is uranium-238*—indistinguishable from U-235 by chemical means, but unable to sustain a chain reaction. Luckily, the percentage of U-235 atoms within a supply of uranium can be increased; but it takes a long, expensive process of step-by-step concentration, or "enrichment."

All ship reactors will probably always need some enrichment. That's because space and weight are limited on board. Higher enrichments reduce the size of the core needed to generate a given amount of power. Besides, reactor fuel which is richer in U-235 will generally last longer. Because compactness and long life are both considered especially important on military ships, all U.S. Navy reactors so far have used uranium which is more than nine-tenths pure U-235. Civilian ships, on the other hand, are more cautious about costs. They usually operate with reactor enrichments of less than five percent.

A single kilogram (2.2 pounds) of uranium in which the U-235 content has been raised to 5 percent costs about $500, even before work begins to manufacture it into a fuel element. Material of "10 percent enrichment" costs a little more than twice that much. Generally, each percentage point of enrichment adds about $100 per kilo to the price—so that uranium enriched to meet military standards is roughly worth its weight in gold.

Like so many other aspects of nuclear propulsion, the "right" enrichment for a particular reactor involves "trade offs" among various advantages and disadvantages.

---

* The number tells how many neutron-sized particles (protons and neutrons) are in each individual atom's nucleus. Only the number of protons affects an atom's chemical nature (*i.e.*, which element it is), but the number of neutrons determines its *nuclear* behavior (whether or not it is radioactive, whether the nucleus may fission, etc.). All uranium atoms have ninety-two protons each, but the number of neutrons varies.

The reactor vessel to hold the power source and steam-generating system for Germany's Otto Hahn *is hoisted aboard (left). It fits inside the containment shell (right), which is surrounded by additional shielding to protect the crew from radiation.*

For instance, a small increase in the size of the core and the equipment closely associated with it can multiply weight considerably. Nuclear ship owners must decide on the exact point at which it becomes too expensive to slim down the power plant further by investing more money in enriching its fuel.

As the dimensions of the nuclear fuel increase, the power plant's total weight is multiplied rapidly by the need to expand the volume of various "layers" around the core. First of all, for safety's sake, a propulsion reactor always operates inside a thick-walled cylinder called a reactor vessel. This normally fits into a larger, gas-tight "containment shell"; and crew members are separated from an operating reactor by a substantial amount of "shielding" as well. Shielding against strong nuclear

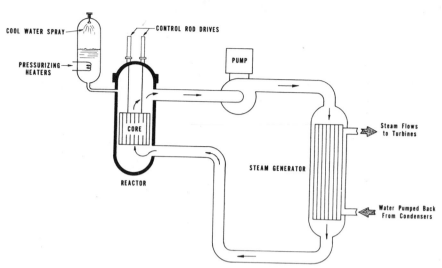

In the most basic shipboard reactor system, control rods are partly withdrawn from among the fuel bundles to turn the reactor on or to increase its power output. Water heated by passing through the core is pumped to a steam generator, where it passes either through or around a cluster of tubes (see photo below). Some of its heat is transmitted through the walls of the metal tubes to a separate supply of water, which is at lower pressure and so turns into steam. Water in the primary part of the reactor system is kept from boiling by a pressurizer. It is adjusted automatically, either by heaters or by a cooling spray, to hold the water pressure constant as reactor power changes.

Aboard Savannah, large pipes enclosed these tubes, which carried water to and from the reactor. Water passing through the large pipes but outside the tubes boiled to produce steam for the ship's turbines. In some other heat exchangers, the water to form the steam goes through thin tubes like these and the reactor water surrounds them; but the principle is the same. The water supplies never mix.

radiation is bulky; it may consist of several feet of concrete, tons of lead plate, water, steel, some plastics, or a combination of all of these materials. On shipboard, some sort of shielding surrounds the reactor completely. Happily, neither the size, the weight, nor the cost of a typical reactor goes up proportionally as its power capacity is increased.

Thousands of different reactor designs are possible. Various combinations of fuel, moderator, and cooling technique can always be used. Hundreds of such designs have actually been developed, at least for study purposes; and dozens have been considered seriously for use in propelling nuclear ships. Yet, with surprisingly slight changes, all shipboard reactors today are still basically the same as the first one in *Nautilus.* The basic type is called a *pressurized-water reactor,* or PWR. Its parts are diagrammed on the opposite page.

In this sort of reactor, very pure water in a "primary system" acts as both a moderator and a coolant for the reactor at the same time. It flows through pipes and passages under such high pressure that it cannot turn to steam even as it goes through the hot core itself, where the water's temperature rises to about 315° C. *Outside* the core, however, the hot, sealed pipes come into contact with a *separate* supply of "secondary" water—which *does* turn into steam because it's under less pressure. Like the reactor coolant, the water in this secondary system is also extremely pure; but the two liquids never touch each other. After the steam has done its work, ordinary sea-water is used to chill it down in the condensers; but no mixing takes place during that heat exchange either.

Obviously, this diagram and several others in this book are greatly simplified. Usually, more than one steam generator is connected to each shipboard reactor. There is also more than one turbine.

33

A photo taken during the construction of Savannah *shows its high-pressure turbine (right rear) and its low-pressure turbine (left rear). Herringbone-patterned reduction gears like those in the foreground change the speed of rotation from several thousand revolutions per minute inside a turbine to about one hundred revolutions per minute for the propeller of a nuclear ship.*

Some turbines can operate more efficiently only while the steam is at its highest pressure. After it has lost some of its energy, the same steam moves along into larger, low-pressure turbines. By then the steam pressure may have dropped to less than one-tenth of what it was when it was first generated; and the blades of these different turbines rotate at different speeds. Nevertheless, matching gear systems make it possible to connect various turbines to the same propeller shaft. Another, completely distinct turbine may operate a special generator to feed electricity to the reactor's own pumps. Still another turbogenerator normally supplies the ship's "hotel load": power for lights, heat, cooking, air conditioning, communications, and anything else apart from actual propulsion. Meanwhile, some steam from the nuclear plant may be used directly—for example, to distill fresh water from the sea or to warm cargo areas.

Commands from the captain aboard a nuclear ship have to be translated into action in many places at once: A reactor operator keeps track of the nuclear steam source through an elaborate console of dials, gauges, switches, and buttons. A different crewman is in charge of directing the steam to the turbines as it is needed—"pouring it on" when the ship is moving at full speed or cutting down the flow at other times. A reactor's operation can be made largely automatic, however. The engine room crew does pretty much the same things it would on a conventional ship, where steam comes from a boiler. The actual steering of the ship, of course, is done from still another area.

Starting a nuclear ship's engine is not quite as easy as turning an auto's ignition key and stepping on the accelerator. On the other hand, it is easier in some ways than the process on other ships of similar size. About four hours before getting under way, a single nuclear specialist begins a routine check of all the reactor control equipment. At the same time, all valves are checked in the reactor compartment and engine room. Two hours later, the areas closest to the reactor core are closed off to all crewmen and the signal is given for the electromagnets or other such devices to begin lifting the control rods slowly. Even while the reactor was shut down, the natural heat of radioactivity (sometimes helped by supplementary heaters) has kept the coolant at a fairly high temperature; so within roughly thirty minutes the reactor should be producing enough additional heat to warm up all the water and steam lines. An hour after that the turbines are ready to begin turning and the turbogenerators are set to be switched on. Then, in fifteen or thirty more minutes, the ship is all ready to leave.

Once a voyage has started, it isn't necessary to shut down the reactor every time the vessel stops. The nuclear power plant usually continues to operate at a low level to take care of the "hotel load." In case the reactor has to shut down for repairs, of course, there are diesel generators aboard (plus batteries on submarines) to handle this job temporarily. They can also supply power to the "take home motors"—which turn the propellers and drive the ship at reduced speed if a serious emergency arises. Incidentally, there are many ways of shutting off a nuclear reactor almost instantly. That's an important part of reactor safety.

Although the descriptions so far fit just about all of today's nuclear ships, technology changes with time. Pressurized-water reactors have worked quite well, yet they have some limitations—even when compared to a conventional ship boiler. For one thing, an oil fire produces usable steam at a much higher temperature than a pressurized-water reactor. The difference is often more than 150°. Hotter steam can drive a turbine more efficiently, and less of the heat is wasted.

Nuclear fission could easily produce higher temperatures, of course—up to millions of degrees. But a reactor has two practical limitations: (1) Unlike wood or coal or oil—all of which burn quickly and then are allowed to turn into ash or tar or sludge—nuclear fuel elements must keep their shape while operating at their peak temperatures for years. As reactor temperatures rise, it's more and more difficult to find materials with which they can be built. (2) It takes a strong pressure vessel to keep water in the primary system under the necessary pressure, even at the fairly low temperatures used now. In-

One of four huge propellers for the carrier Enterprise is fitted onto its drive shaft. The picture below gives an even better idea of its size.

The engine room of the Russian icebreaker Lenin *looks a lot like one aboard a nonnuclear vessel. Basically, steam is still what drives the ship.*

creasing the water temperature (and thus the pressure) would be too difficult and too costly to be worthwhile.

Many nuclear power plants on shore get a slightly higher temperature from nuclear reactors by allowing the "primary" water to boil and turn to steam itself. Such "boiling-water reactors" would be far harder to control on a rolling, pitching ship at sea, however. The moderating effect of the water in the core would tend to be uneven as it sloshed around. Furthermore, steam isn't nearly as good a coolant as hot water (even at a similar temperature), and if a pocket of steam should form more than momentarily near a fuel element the heat of the operating reactor might burn right through the cladding. There are other problems as well. Control rods for this type of reactor normally must enter the core from the bottom, but that forces the heaviest part of the reactor upward—making it annoyingly topheavy, in the opinion of most ship architects. Furthermore, a boiling-water reactor (or "BWR") usually transmits radioactivity to the turbines through its steam, so that it would be virtually impossible to make even minor repairs to the turbine at sea. A leak in the condensers (which isn't too unusual aboard ship) could spread radioactivity further by activating the minerals in the seawater used for cooling. Finally, a BWR produces slightly radioactive waste gases which have to be released periodically. Not much radioactivity is involved in this "venting," but sensitive monitors on the surface could track it. No military submarine wants to leave a trail like this behind it, and the overwhelming majority of nuclear ships built so far *are* military submarines.

Another way of increasing the temperature of a shipboard reactor would be to use some coolant fluid other than water—one which can be heated to substantially higher temperatures without needing so much pressure to keep it in check. This method *has* been tried, although the results weren't very encouraging.

The steering station on a modern nuclear submarine resembles an airplane's cockpit. This one is French.

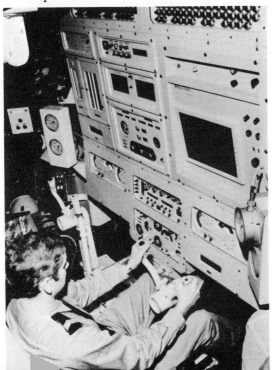

The second U.S. nuclear submarine, *Seawolf*, used molten sodium metal to cool its original reactor core. A solid material, beryllium, was used as the moderator. Pipes containing the liquid sodium passed through one section of a double heat exchange system and then back into the reactor. The reactor's heat was transferred first to a molten mixture of sodium and potassium, and then to a separate supply of water. This water was turned into steam to feed the turbines; and from that point on the system was just like the one which *Nautilus* had pioneered. The reason for using sodium and the sodium-potassium alloy was that both metals melt at less than 100°C. Even without being pressurized, they can be heated to nearly 900°C. without boiling. They pick up heat quickly and pass it along efficiently through the heat exchanger.

Unfortunately, however, sodium becomes more highly radioactive than water as it circulates through a reactor, so heavier shielding is needed. Besides, either sodium or potassium can react with water to produce a chemical explosion. *Seawolf*'s reactor system was troubled from the start with minor leaks, and the Navy was afraid that the sub might develop a serious problem while it was far from any port where it could seek help. The experiment was scrapped after less than two years, and *Seawolf* was reequipped with a pressurized-water reactor. The radioactive reactor vessel and other useless components from *Seawolf*'s original plant were welded inside a steel barge, which was scuttled during the spring of 1959 in deep water more than 100 miles off the New Jersey coast.

There is no reason why other types of reactors—and even other systems of nuclear propulsion—shouldn't be tried, however. As far back as 1966, the U.S. Navy began testing a "natural circulation reactor," which was installed experimentally on the submarine *Narwhal* in

The U.S. Navy submarine Narwhal.

1969. This reactor works without any big pumps in its primary loop, relying on temperature differences within the water to cause coolant to flow in the right direction. "Quiet" submarines now planned will also use another basic change to reduce operating noises; they will turn their propellers by electric motors—eliminating the reduction gears. Other changes within the next twenty-five or thirty years are likely to be even more radical, as we'll see later on.

Is it worth all this effort? Wouldn't it be simpler to stick with ships that burn the so-called fossil fuels—coal, oil, and gas? Those ships are cheaper and quicker to build than the "nukes." They're less complicated, too. Why bother with nuclear propulsion?

The answers to those questions are the basis of the next chapter.

CHAPTER THREE

Why Nuclear Propulsion?

M ost nuclear submarines are big and fast. They are mobile launching pads for giant missiles. Yet that isn't enough to distinguish them from the "old-fashioned" submarines of twenty or thirty years ago. Some of those were big and fast and versatile, too.

The Japanese had subs during the 1940's which were almost as big as *Triton*. They were 400-foot-long monsters that carried fully assembled seaplanes. Before *Nautilus* ever put out to sea, a nonnuclear British submarine had reached a top speed close to 30 knots. Earlier, Nazi Germany had even started to build ballistic-missile "trailers" in which its U-boats hoped to tow V-2 rockets into launching range so they could be fired at the East Coast of the United States. So why was nuclear propulsion considered such a revolutionary development? What did it add?

Nuclear power plants gave submarines *independence*. Atomic subs don't need to surface for air; they have machinery that "scrubs" the air clean after it has been used, so that it can be used again. With enough fuel on board to last for years, a submarine commander can cruise at full speed constantly—without any danger of "running out of gas." So much energy is available, in fact, that an A-

Men on the deck and conning tower of one of the airplane-carrying submarines used by the Japanese during World War II (above) show how enormous it was. Yet it could travel only about 60 miles without surfacing. It took nuclear-propelled subs like Skate (below) to traverse the Arctic Ocean—an ice-covered area larger than the United States.

sub can afford to carry all sorts of extra equipment. Some of this just makes life on the submarine more pleasant; other parts of it help in performing new and complicated jobs.

Before nuclear power was introduced, submarines had to spend most of their time on the surface. They could dive out of sight briefly. During World War II some German subs even ducked under the edge of the Arctic ice occasionally to hide. But they couldn't survive for much more than a day without fresh air, even if they remained perfectly still. Even the giant Japanese subs couldn't travel submerged for much more than half a day at a time—and then they had to cut their speed back to a few knots. Any engine that burns conventional fuel uses up oxygen rapidly. Batteries can do without it, but they lose their charge quickly when they have to drive an entire vessel.

Starting in the 1930's, German engineers experimented with chemicals that could *store* oxygen aboard a submarine, such as hydrogen peroxide. They tried the same technique with rockets; and the general principle is still used on space flights (chemical rockets carry an *oxidizer* in addition to their fuel). Nevertheless, the endurance of such submarines was always limited by the bulk and weight of their propellants. A rocket engine normally needs to operate for only a few minutes at a time in space; the diesel-oil-and-peroxide subs could keep their turbines spinning at high speed under water for no more than five or six hours at a stretch.

Another way to give conventional submarines more freedom of movement was the "snorkel." This is a retractable tube that connects the sub with air on the surface. The Germans and Japanese used snorkels often during the 1940's, and the Soviet Union's postwar fleet relied on them heavily. Once again, however, there were serious drawbacks. The small breathing tube at the surface could be seen, so the submarine could be spotted and tracked by planes or other ships. Besides, a sub had to stay fairly close to the surface while operating its snorkel. In a way, it was like trying to fly an airplane with an extension cord attached. Most important of all, however, a snorkel submarine still had a restricted operating range. It could travel only as far as a single load of chemical propellants would drive it. Then it had to refuel somewhere.

With all these things in mind, it seems that conventionally fueled "submarines" barely deserved the name, at least as we use it today. They were simply "boats that could submerge." Their hulls were designed for the most part like surface vessels'—with sharp bows to reduce "drag" along the line where air and water meet as a ship moves along the surface. *Nautilus* was the first vessel in history to *live* under water like a fish. It's not surprising that it touched off a new trend in naval architecture; later nuclear submarines came to be *shaped* more like undersea creatures. This idea wasn't wholly new, however. Crude nineteenth-century subs had been modeled after fish, and Jules Verne's fictional *Nautilus* was shaped somewhat like a whale.

New types of streamlining, which had been tested earlier by an experimental diesel submarine called *Albacore,* increased the speed and maneuverability of new nuclear subs. By diving to greater depths, they soon multiplied the space in which they could operate. Guidance systems which had been developed originally for missiles enabled the subs to navigate without ever surfacing to check their positions by the stars. Rockets were designed so that they could be fired by nuclear subs from underwater hiding places toward either land or sea targets. The nuclear submarine was more than just a ship with a new type of propulsion unit; it was a brand-new creature.

As far back as 1939, Dr. Ross Gunn and other scientists

The hulls of Seawolf and Nautilus, the first two nuclear subs (above) were similar to those of older diesels. Because it can spend most of its time under water, however, a nuclear sub doesn't need a sharp bow to cut through surface waves. As the launching photo of the Flying Fish (below) shows, styles changed.

at the Naval Research Laboratory in Washington had understood that nuclear-powered submarines could change naval strategy and tactics as much as they had been changed when steam engines replaced sails on surface vessels. Nuclear reactors were only a theoretical possibility then. Nobody had tried to build one, and no one yet knew how to "enrich" uranium. But naval experts were sure that a *true* submarine (one that could operate almost indefinitely in the depths of the sea) would be a totally different sort of weapon from any that existed at that time. It's not strange that nuclear propulsion eventually caused the U.S. Navy to modify one old habit. Officers and sailors had always referred to a submarine —no matter how big it might be—as a boat. Now they are instructed officially to speak of nuclear subs as ships.

What about nuclear-powered warships aside from submarines, though? And what about *peaceful* uses of nuclear maritime propulsion? The advantages there don't seem as clear. Exactly what are they?

First, let's take a look at surface warships, and then at commercial nukes. A good place to start is with the aircraft carriers. *Nimitz*, for example, is more than a floating air base. She can do things that a nonnuclear aircraft carrier of the same size cannot, because nuclear power enables the ship to make some of her own ground rules for the way she operates.

Most aircraft can't take off from (or land on) a carrier when the air on the flight deck is dead calm. A breeze from the right direction is needed to help lift the plane for a quick takeoff as the catapult hurls it down its short, seaborne runway. The wind can also help a plane slow itself to safe landing speed as it nears the deck with its flaps down. At times, any carrier must adjust the speed and direction of wind along its deck by changing the direction and speed of the ship itself; but nuclear power

Jets line up at two launching catapults aboard Enterprise. *Nuclear carriers can put their planes into the air faster than their conventional sister ships.*

makes this easier. Increasing or decreasing the power output of a nuclear reactor is as easy as pushing a switch. Control rods move out or in, and the power change is virtually instantaneous.*

No oil-fired carrier can accelerate or decelerate so rapidly; so none can match the smooth, continuous operation of ships like *Enterprise, Nimitz,* and *Eisenhower.* Their ability to maneuver is especially helpful when a carrier is using both helicopters and fixed-wing aircraft.

---

* Nuclear physics adds a further explanation of why the power plant responds to those orders so well. For several reasons, most shipboard reactors are designed to have a "negative temperature coefficient." This means that as the temperature goes *up* the nuclear fission process *slows down* somewhat. On the other hand, as temperature *drops* the rate of fission *increases*. Thus, whenever a ship's engineers draw off heat more rapidly to provide additional steam the reactor automatically perks up. For small changes, it may not even be necessary to shift the control rods.

The "choppers" don't like wind, even though the regular airplanes need it. A nuclear carrier can shift its deck wind rapidly enough to accommodate both in rapid succession.

Nuclear power shows another advantage for flight operations when there is *no* wind. At times like that, a carrier must steam ahead at 35 knots—just about full speed—to produce enough movement along the deck to launch or recover certain types of planes at all. It still needs its catapults, however; and those are powered by steam. If most of the steam available from the ship's boilers is being fed into the propulsion turbines, the catapults will have to slow up their operations to let steam pressure build up again. A delay of ten to twenty seconds between launches may not seem like much, but precious minutes slip away quickly when a carrier is trying to release its entire flock of perhaps one hundred planes.

Nuclear reactors on a ship provide extra power (either steam *or* electricity) whenever it's needed. As a result, the nukes are also able to use a tremendous array of sophisticated electronic gadgetry without any strain. A nuclear carrier, for example, carries about five hundred antennas, ranging from tiny ones (weighing less than a pound each) to giants which tip the scales at more than eighteen tons apiece. The "hotel load" alone on the carrier *Nimitz* is roughly equal to the power supply for a city of 50,000, even though the ship and plane crews aboard total only about 6,300 men. If *all* of the ship's power were to be turned into electricity, its two reactors could supply the daily needs of a city of about 200,000 people.

Nuclear ships aren't necessarily faster than conventional ones. As Chapter Two pointed out, steam from an oil-burning boiler can easily produce a combination of higher temperature and higher pressure than the steam

49

from current nuclear reactors. A conventional aircraft carrier might beat a nuke in a short sprint. The problem for the oil-burner is that it can't afford to maintain the pace. Continuous speed is extremely expensive in the amount of energy it takes. A nonnuclear carrier like *John F. Kennedy* will be down to its emergency fuel reserves after only a couple of days of high-speed steaming, and refueling takes time—even when done at sea. Thus, nuclear power chops two days off the time a carrier takes to cross the Atlantic; and it can save nearly a week on a

Powerful "billboard-type" radar antennas surround the relatively small island on a nuclear carrier. The absence of smokestacks offers many advantages.

Pacific crossing. Furthermore, the nuke is ready for action as soon as it arrives. No group of conventional ships in the world could have kept up with *Enterprise, Bainbridge,* and *Long Beach* when they circled the earth together in 1964. They completed the trip in sixty-five days, completely free of refueling or any other logistical support. That demonstration voyage was called Operation Sea Orbit. The nuclear task force traveled at speeds of over 25 knots in all kinds of weather—even in a sixteen-hour gale off the tip of South America and while passing through the Indian Ocean during the monsoon season. The cruise showed that naval power would no longer have to depend so heavily on bases all around the world.

Indirectly, Operation Sea Orbit also showed that big nuclear-propelled surface warships would be slowed down unless other ships traveling with them had the same independence. Not as many fuel-carrying escort vessels are needed in an atomic task force, of course; but this has probably been the strongest argument for building nuclear-powered frigates like *Truxtun, California, South Carolina, Virginia,* and the other small nuclear ships to follow.

Fuel oil for a major warship takes up lots of room on board. In its place, a nuclear aircraft carrier can store about a dozen additional planes, nearly twice as much aviation fuel, and 50 percent more ammunition. When those supplies *do* run low (as they did every few days during Vietnam operations), a nuclear carrier can stick to its station longer than a conventional carrier, too. The captain of the nuclear ship knows that he will need less time to visit a friendly port or to rendezvous with resupply ships at sea; nuclear power permits him to go and return at top speed.

A nuclear ship has more usable room on its decks, as

well as down below. It needs no air intakes or smoke-stacks for the boilers, so the "island" on the main deck is smaller. Furthermore, if there are no smokestacks, there are no exhaust gases. That makes accompanying helicopter and plane pilots much happier. Smoke sometimes makes it hard to see; hot gases may cause tricky and dangerous air currents.

The exhaust fumes from oil-fueled boilers are dirty, too, and when they mix with salty sea air they cause corrosion. Nuclear ships have fewer problems in protecting sensitive radar antennas and communication equipment from the effects of such air pollution. The skipper of *Bainbridge* once reported proudly that his crew was able to devote 440 man-hours per week to other, more important duties because the customary "soot-and-grime detail" could be reduced.

The speed and endurance of nuclear surface ships makes them less vulnerable—either to human enemies or to bad weather. One of the greatest threats from either source comes when a ship is refueling. Nuclear power cuts that danger considerably. With the luxury of an almost unlimited energy source, a nuke can go around the worst storms. It can also avoid hostile ships if necessary—and even evade an enemy nuclear sub. To reach top speed, nuclear submarines can't avoid making noise. However, that interferes with the sub's own sonar. It also makes the sub "visible" to listening devices. That reduces its normal advantage of concealment if a high-speed chase should develop.

In case of an aerial attack, reactor-powered surface ships have one more unusual but important defense. They can "button up" to safeguard themselves against radioactive fallout from nuclear explosions. With no need to draw in air for their steam boilers, nuclear ships can seal themselves off rather effectively from any kind of

Bainbridge has just zigzagged rapidly and washed down her decks, practicing what she would do in case of a nuclear bomb or missile attack. Radioactive fallout is more of a threat to conventional ships because they must take in air constantly for the boilers.

contamination in the atmosphere. This wouldn't help in case of a direct hit by a large nuclear warhead, but at least it would mean vital protection from the devastating side effects of a near miss. In wartime, ships would stay far apart. Spread out in an area the size of the state of New York, a handful of nuclear ships could work together yet still offer a tough target.

Most of the advantages cited so far relate to war, but measuring sticks in the business world are different. That's why commercial nuclear vessels have been slower to appear.

A freight shipping line has less need for extra energy on board. It doesn't equip its fleet with plane catapults, superspecial radar, ultrasensitive communication equipment, and missile-firing systems. The captain of a tanker might *like* the greater maneuverability of a nuclear ship, but he *can* get along without it. Even the *endurance* of nuclear ships is unnecessary for most commercial voyages. A round-the-world luxury cruise would be pointless if it didn't stop at a number of ports; there are frequent opportunities to refuel.

The questions commercial shipowners ask about a new vessel design are different from the ones military men propose. Most businessmen merely want to know how much a ship will be able to deliver and how successfully its profits can pay off their investment. There have not been many cases where nuclear power could give them the kinds of answers they want, although the number is increasing.

In one way nuclear merchant ships *are* like the Navy's aircraft carriers. They can certainly use the enormous space that a regular oil-burner would have needed for its own fuel. Without increasing a ship's overall size, the use of nuclear propulsion *can* leave room for more cargo, and/or passengers. That means added income.

The dimensions of the power plant itself have to be considered also, however. The spread-out design used aboard *Savannah*, for instance, was simple but wasteful. That first nuclear merchant ship's power plant was considerably larger than ordinary boilers of the same steam capacity would have been. Counting all its safety shields, the nuclear plant *weighed* approximately as much as the fuel oil it replaced. As Chapter Five will explain, however, the nuclear layout for the ore ship *Otto Hahn* shows that this problem can be solved—even without resorting to a more expensive form of nuclear fuel. On large com-

Slightly more than 4,000,000 barrels of conventional ship fuel

Nuclear reactor, fully fueled •

The big drum represents the total space which would be taken up by the fuel used during five years' operation of a ship with 120,000 shaft horsepower. The small black cylinder shows the size of a nuclear steam source, equipped with a five-year reactor core to do the same propulsion job.

mercial nuclear ships in the future, the steam source should be slightly smaller than comparable boilers. Every bit of the unneeded "fuel space" will be a bonus for the ships' operators. Reactor weight will be less of a problem, too, because weight depends on the volume of the reactor rather than on its power output.

There is another way to deliver more cargo, too. A ship can simply make more trips. Civilian ships must pay the same penalty as military ships when it comes to speed, however. It takes an enormous amount of additional energy to speed up even a little. The luxury liner *United States* had to gulp down about 50 tons of black oil each hour in order to make its record dash across the Atlantic in three and a half days.

A supertanker delivering fuel oil which wanted to speed up from 15 or 16 knots to 24 knots might find that haste makes waste. It could use up between one-sixth and one-third of the cargo it was carrying, just to make the trip.

Ships are rated by "shaft horsepower" (abbreviated as shp); and this indicates the peak amount of energy they devote to propelling themselves. If a surface ship of a certain size, type, and loading needs 15,000 shaft horse-power for a top speed of 15 knots, it theoretically takes about 120,000 shp—*eight times as much*—to get up to 30 knots. That may be totally uneconomical for a ship that burns oil; it may also be wholly impractical (because of the fuel space needed) for some long voyages. This is where nuclear power can pay off for business shipping—propelling *large* ships at *high* speeds, especially on routes which involve great distances between the ports of call. To multiply a *nuclear* ship's shaft horsepower by eight, you might only have to double the power plant's size and triple its weight. And, of course, this would include a full fuel supply for many months.

A nuclear reactor costs far more to build than a ship boiler that uses fossil fuel. Overall construction of the nuclear ship is more expensive, too, because of extra protection against collision damage and other special requirements. But once it is there, a nuclear power plant

The outline of a modern nuclear steam source for a big cargo liner shows that it would actually be smaller than the two conventional ship boilers (shaded area) it is designed to replace.

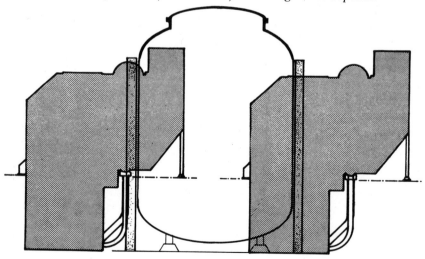

Commercial cargo subs are being planned to follow routes across the top of the world charted by military craft like Whale, *whose superstructure is mirrored in the sunglasses of its commander.*

turns out energy at a fraction of the cost of oil or gas. This advantage in operating costs grew rapidly around the beginning of the 1970's. That's when fossil fuel prices doubled within a few years, while nuclear fuel prices leveled off. At the same time there was a sudden new demand for big, fast ships. The speed of the giant new cargo liners being ordered at the beginning of this decade averaged more than 50 percent greater than comparable ship types in the mid-1960's. Today, more than forty ships of 80,000 shp or more are being built. With oil costing more than $3 per barrel, some of those big new ships could save as much as $3,000,000 a year by using nuclear fuel instead of oil. *Some* of them *will*.

Still, nuclear ships save money in this way only while they are *moving*. Their days in port don't give them any opportunity to make up for the higher initial cost which an owner has already paid out. For that reason, the prospects of peaceful nuclear shipping are also linked to any developments which let merchant ships spend more of their time in motion. Faster methods of loading and unloading are obviously important. So is the expansion of trade along the long routes from Europe and the United States to Asia and the Southern Hemisphere. The speediest merchant ships operating today must slow down on such voyages to avoid running out of fuel along the way.

Finally, however, there is one special way in which nuclear-propelled ships are likely to *shorten* trade routes. That's by following the trails opened by military subs or by the high-powered nuclear icebreaker *Lenin* in the Arctic. Even a surface voyage through the icy waters can cut travel time considerably between the Atlantic and the Pacific oceans. But hauling cargo *under* the ice sheet would be even more direct. Going across the top of the world would be like bringing London and Tokyo 5,000 miles (about 7,500 kilometers) closer together.

Commercial subs could look forward to smooth voyages, too. One great asset of taking long cruises under water is often overlooked: You avoid all storms!

CHAPTER FOUR

A Look at Four Nuclear Navies

In 1965 about two-thirds of the world's nuclear war-ships still carried the American flag. A few years later, the United States' share had dropped below three-out-of-five. By 1971 there were more nuclear warships in foreign fleets than in the U.S. Navy.

The trend will probably continue, although not as sharply. Naval shipyards of Great Britain, France, and the USSR are likely to produce nuclear ships steadily at a combined rate which is higher than that in the United States. China will have to be considered, too. Reports from the mainland have hinted since the mid-1960's that nuclear ships were being planned or actually built there; and in 1971 aerial photos showed the distinctive hull of a small nuclear sub in a Chinese shipyard. The four nuclear navies of today will almost surely increase to five by the middle of this decade.

Icebreakers like the Soviet Union's *Lenin* and *Arktika* might be considered part of the Russian Navy, but they are not built for fighting. Neither is the Japanese training ship *Mutsu*. Like the U.S. Navy's deep-diving research sub (which has no name, but only the designation NR-1), those ships will be treated separately in the next chapter, "The Peaceful Ones." This chapter will stick to

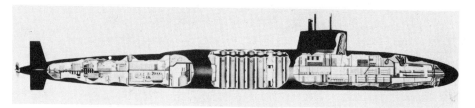

(Above) a missile-firing submarine of the U.S. Navy, Daniel Boone *(SSBN-629). (Below) a cutaway diagram.*

a comparison of American, Russian, British, and French *submarines*—and a description of U.S. surface ships which are clearly *military* nukes.

The United States is less secretive than most countries about its nuclear navy, so a lot of information about its subs can be pieced together from official sources. In fact, many people—including Admiral Rickover—argue that the United States reveals too much about its fleet. The admiral was indignant when accurate scale models of our nuclear fighting ships were put on sale at drugstores and supermarkets in "build-them-yourself" kits.

Democracy works best, however, when citizens are well

informed. That's why many details in the following pages could be discovered by a careful reading of Congressional hearings. These are public reports, released only after Navy officials have had a chance to eliminate the facts they consider military secrets. Sometimes, though, this leaves the reader frustrated and confused—as in the case of the following description of a new project:

> *Admiral Rickover.* We are designing it to be as quiet as we know how. We estimate it should be about [deleted] as the latest class of submarines we are about to lay down. [Deleted].
>
> *Representative Holifield.* Is it your opinion it will be as [deleted]?
>
> *Admiral Rickover.* No submarine is [deleted]. There is little you can do [deleted]. The only time you can get [deleted]. In this connection the Electric Drive submarine is expected to be [deleted] than the submarines we are about to lay down.

This book won't try to fill in all those blanks. It *will* include a few "educated guesses" which can't be checked because of military security rules. For the most part, it will be a reliable picture.

After the instant success of *Nautilus*, the world's first nuclear submarine, the U.S. Navy and the U.S. Atomic Energy Commission pushed ahead with half a dozen additional experiments. Some were more successful than others, but each was important in its own way. In fact, the entire early history of nuclear subs can be summarized in the stories of just six vessels: *Seawolf, Triton, Halibut, Skate, Skipjack,* and *Tullibee.*

Seawolf—SSN 575

This sub was described on page 40 in Chapter Two. Construction began on *Seawolf* in September, 1953— almost a year and a half before *Nautilus* first put to sea. Nobody was sure then whether water or liquid metal

Some pioneer nukes: *(Above)*, Nautilus; *(below)*, Seawolf; *(opposite top)*, Triton; *(middle)*, Halibut; *(bottom)*, Tullibee.

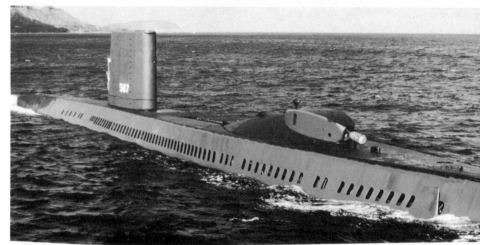

would do a better all-around job as a reactor coolant; and quite a few experts thought that metal-cooled *Seawolf* might make water-cooled *Nautilus* obsolete immediately. As it turned out, *Nautilus'* pressurized-water reactor worked fine, but *Seawolf's* molten metal system developed leaks. The original *Seawolf* approach was dropped then, but it had not been a waste of time. The sodium-cooled reactor actually propelled *Seawolf* farther than the 20,000 leagues (60,000 miles, or nearly 100,000 kilometers) covered by Jules Verne's fictional submarine. Its engineering logs were studied long after the original reactor was replaced. Just as the Navy's experience with PWR's helped to produce the United States' first commercial nuclear power plant at Shippingport, Pennsylvania, some lessons from *Seawolf* were eventually useful on land. Work with liquid-metal-cooled reactors continued; and more than twenty years later this technique is to be included in a revolutionary "breeder" reactor in Tennessee—where a power plant is expected to produce fissionable nuclear fuel faster than it uses up its original supply.

Triton—SSN 586

About the time *Seawolf* was launched, work began on a more powerful pressurized-water reactor. It was a test model for the *two* reactors which would be installed in a thoroughly new type of ship—*Triton*. This was to be the largest submersible ever built, with a 170-man crew.

Triton was 447 feet long (more than 136 meters), or nearly half again the length of *Nautilus*. Completely submerged, the ship displaced about 7,800 tons of water.*

---

* "Tonnage" may mean several different things when applied to ships. *Displacement tonnage* (which is being used here) is just what it sounds like—the weight of seawater which would occupy the exact space taken up by a ship as it floats or moves through the ocean. When a ship is on the surface, this is the same as the reading you would get if you could hoist the ship itself onto a big

Strangely, however, *Triton* was designed to do a large part of its work on the surface. Unlike other nuclear subs, this one was faster there than underwater. The twin steam power plants turned two oversized bronze propellers, which allowed *Triton* to keep up with an aircraft carrier task force at a steady clip of about 27 knots. Its almost limitless supply of electrical energy powered radar equipment, which gave the whole surface force unusually sharp "eyes." *Triton* could dive out of sight, however, if an enemy attacked.

Considering its design and mission, it is odd that *Triton* is remembered best now for being the first vessel in history to go all the way around the globe without surfacing. This was done on its first, "shakedown" cruise; and the feat achieved its aim of impressing the world.

Within a few years the Navy decided it would be better to let regular surface vessels do the radar job intended for *Triton*, and the big ship was reclassified as an "attack" submarine. Its shape slowed it down underwater, though. In spite of the two big reactors, *Triton* probably would not have been able to keep pace with *Nautilus*. It surely couldn't match the newer and faster nukes. No "sister ships" for *Triton* were ever ordered; and the sub was retired from service in 1969.

Halibut—SSN 587

Torpedoes and deck guns were the chief weapons used

---

scale. That measurement for *Triton* was a bit less than 6,000 tons. Obviously, *Triton* displaced more water than that when it filled its ballast tanks and submerged.

Deadweight tonnage is another measurement of weight, used mainly for merchant ships. It is the difference between the displacement of the empty ship and the weight of the water it displaces when fully loaded.

Gross tonnage is not really a measurement of weight at all. It indicates the amount of space enclosed within a vessel, with each 100 cubic feet estimated as equaling one ton.

Net tonnage represents space on a ship in the same way, but it is limited to cargo-carrying space.

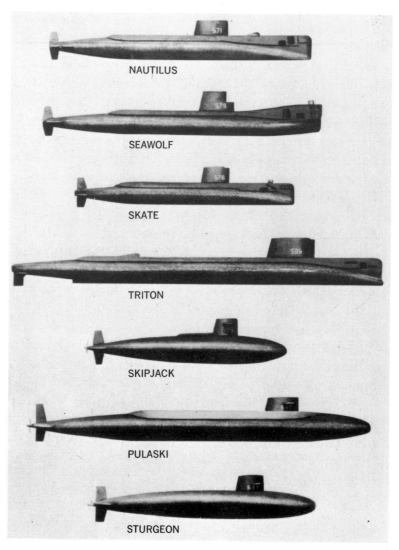

Silhouettes show the changing shapes of U.S. nuclear submarines.

on old-fashioned submarines. Nukes appeared at a time when sophisticated new missiles were being developed. It was natural for the U.S. Navy to look for a way of putting the two together.

Halibut was sort of a submersible aircraft carrier, but it carried guided missiles rather than piloted aircraft.

The five Regulus missiles aboard were winged, air-breathing jets, not rockets. They could be fired only while *Halibut* was on the surface. The superstructure of the sub (called the sail) was built far aft (toward the ship's stern). That provided more space on the broad forward part of the hull for launching operations. A large "missile hangar" was clearly visible on the bow.

Halibut was roomier than the diesel subs which were also modified to carry guided missiles of this type during the late 1950's and early 1960's. *Halibut* was also slightly faster than they were underwater, but it was a relative slowpoke on the surface. That didn't matter much; the important thing was for *Halibut* to provide a steady launch platform if the nuclear-warhead missiles had to be fired.

Once again, quick changes in technology left a nuclear sub without a job. Ballistic rocket missiles soon came to be favored over the slower, air-breathing "cruise missiles" like Regulus. The military milestone marked by *Halibut* was simply that subs after it would definitely be used to carry long-range weapons.

Halibut's design was never duplicated in another ship, but it was succeeded by several new series of missile-firing nukes. The thinking behind *Halibut* spawned weapon ideas like Polaris, Poseidon, and the newest missiles in the Trident program.

Meanwhile, *Halibut* shed her teeth. With the outmoded missiles removed, its spacious interior could accommodate the equipment needed in ocean research projects. Along with old *Seawolf*, this sub was turned into a mother ship for deep-diving Navy experimental vehicles.

Skate—SSN 578

Almost as soon as *Nautilus* finished sea trials and was

67

accepted by the Navy, construction began on standardized production models. The four submarines of the *Skate* class are noticeably smaller and lighter than *Nautilus*. Their power plants are simpler, and their machinery is easier to reach for maintenance. *Skate*'s reactor is identical to the one aboard *Halibut*; but the trimmer design of the *Skate* class made them faster.

Skate, Swordfish, Sargo, and *Seadragon* entered service between December, 1957, and December, 1959. Although *Nautilus* was the pioneer in underwater polar travel, these first production subs quickly became the great Arctic explorers. They crisscrossed the ice pack in winter as well as summer. They punched holes through the ice with their sails in order to surface. They showed that subs could meet and work together in the Far North. They also charted the Arctic sea floor extensively. Using extra sonar detectors pointing upward to bounce sound waves off the bottoms of deep-floating icebergs, they threaded their way through amazingly shallow passages, sometimes with only a few feet to spare between ice and ocean bed.

Even within this small group of subs, improvements were made between one ship and the next. On *Seadragon* and *Swordfish*, parts of the nuclear power plant were spread out in the hull. Crewmen serviced them from within a long, shielded tunnel. Aboard *Sargo* and *Skate*, all the radioactive components were laid out beneath a shielded deck so that the men could walk about above them at will.

Nuclear submarines were finally beginning a major role with the U.S. fleet. They had proved their practicality and endurance, and planners decided to concentrate still more on speed.

Skipjack—SSN 585

Even before work got under way on the final submarine of the *Skate* class, the keel was laid for the first of
six subs in a faster series. A slightly better reactor was
ready by then, and for the first time a nuclear sub was
built so that all of its propulsive power could be fed to a
single, five-bladed propeller. Earlier nukes had split the
output from a single reactor between two propeller
shafts, but that method was less efficient.

Skipjack and her five sister-subs had a new silhouette,
too. They were smoothly rounded, and each one tapered
toward the tail. The strangely bulbous bow didn't seem
graceful to most people at first, but this new shape had
been developed after years of tests with an experimental
diesel-powered sub called *Albacore*. It worked.

Projections from the outside of the hull were kept to a
minimum, and they were streamlined. Deck cleats and
some other items which are needed only while the sub is
on the surface were designed to fold inward when traveling submerged. It was harder to stand on the outside
deck of a submarine like this, because the upper hull is
curved instead of being flat. These subs were supposed to
spend almost all of their time underwater, and that's
where they could outrun or overtake anything else in the
sea. *Skipjack* was the first submarine to exceed 30 knots
continuously, and its top speed was probably closer to 35
before various sorts of new equipment were added and its
weight increased.

Tullibee—SSN 597

The wartime job of an "attack submarine" is to cap-
ture, disable, or sink ships. To do that, it has to *find* the
enemy ships. Furthermore, it must try to keep from being
detected and destroyed by the other side. A submerged
submarine "hears" ships with its sonar equipment; so the

less noise a sub makes itself, the keener its hearing will be and the less risk it runs of being spotted by an unfriendly ship. *Tullibee* was the first full-fledged experiment to improve nuclear submarines in regard to underwater sound.

Tullibee is the smallest nuclear warship ever built by the United States. It is five feet longer than the *Skate* class, but slim *Tullibee* displaces about 200 tons less when submerged. *Tullibee* is far less powerful, so it isn't nearly as fast. But it is quiet, and it hears very well.

Sonar domes project from the hull; *Tullibee*'s snub nose is jammed with electronic listening systems. Some observers say that *Tullibee* can hear a door closing aboard another submarine several miles away.

Tullibee eliminates the noise of reduction gears (described and pictured in Chapter Two) because it operates without them. Instead, *Tullibee*'s small nuclear reactor generates electricity for a motor, which turns its single propeller.

Turbine-electric-drive propulsion was used on the big old French liner *Normandie*, and it was also used during World War II on some large U.S. Navy ships—carriers and battleships. Such earlier equipment was rebuilt in miniature and installed on *Tullibee* for experimental purposes. Later it would be used on a much larger scale in the Navy's first new, quiet-design sub, *Glenard P. Lipscomb*. Some of the original heat energy is lost by converting it into electricity first and then changing that into energy-of-motion; so a turbine-electric sub must trade part of its power (and thus speed) for its ability to cruise about with less telltale noise.

The six types of submarines mentioned so far as successors to *Nautilus* account for most of the early developments in the U.S. Nuclear Navy. All together, however, they involved only fourteen vessels in what was destined

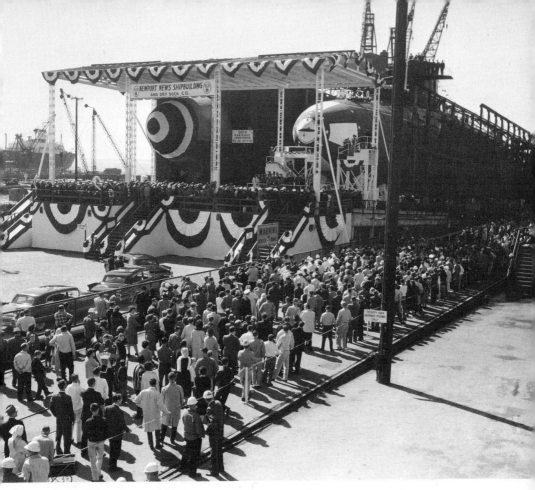

Missile subs have grown longer and heavier. James Monroe *(left) juts out over the platform during the launching ceremony for* Thomas Jefferson *(right).*

to become a fleet of well over one hundred nuclear submarines. Many changes have taken place since then, but all other American war-subs fall into just two categories. Either they are intended to fire long-range missiles, or they are designed as "killer subs" to fight other ships—a duty in which both speed and quiet are important.

The first of the ballistic missile subs was *George Washington*, and it is an old-timer in service as well as in name. As a result of a remarkably rapid development program, this ship was commissioned on the day before New Year's Eve in 1959.

71

The Navy's Viking program had shown it was possible to fire large, liquid-propellant rockets from shipboard; yet it seemed clear that rocket weapons for submarines should rely on solid fuel. Solids were easier to handle and simpler to launch. One early idea was to carry rockets on the outside of a sub. The sub could release the missiles with floats, then fire them by remote control after they had bobbed to the surface. But missiles sticking out all over a sub were bound to slow it down, so the suggestion was scrapped.

The order was given near the end of 1955 to develop a missile which could be fired from inside a nuclear submarine while it was still submerged. The rocket was supposed to be accurate in reaching a target 1,500 miles (about 2,500 kilometers) away. Many officials thought the project would take more than ten years, but it was speeded up after the Russians launched Sputnik I in 1957. The result of the crash effort was the Polaris missile. The job was done so quickly that unusual steps had to be taken to provide nuclear subs to carry it as soon as Polaris was ready.

The keel had been laid for a *Skipjack*-class submarine called *Scorpion*.* When the rush order came, that hull was cut in half and a new center section was inserted to provide room for sixteen Polaris launching tubes. The vessel was redesignated *George Washington*, because officials thought that such an important class of ships should bear the names of great men. Its numerical designation was switched to SSBN 598 (with the *B* indicating that the vessel is primarily a ballistic missile launcher).

With its new 130-foot center section and a load of missiles, *George Washington* displaced nearly as much tonnage on the surface as the whopping *Triton*. A 1,200-mile

---

* The name *Scorpion* was reassigned to another *Skipjack*-class attack submarine, on which construction began in August, 1958. Approximately ten years later, that sub was lost in the Atlantic.

version of Polaris had already been test-fired successfully from a rocking, pitching platform on land—which simulated the motion of a sub at sea. Dummy missiles had already been popped to the surface by compressed gas to show that underwater launchings from a sub were possible. Finally, on July 20, 1960, all the pieces of the complex project came together. From beneath the surface, off the coast of Florida, *George Washington* let go with two missiles. Each Polaris broke into the open, ignited its rocket motor, and roared off to the southeast along the Atlantic Missile Test Range. The Fleet Ballistic Missile submarine (or FBM) had been born.

Four other FBM's were built to the same specifications, and all of them were ready for duty by early 1961. These were followed by two other classes of similar submarines, but the later ones were designed from the beginning to be missile launchers.

Each new group was longer and heavier than the last. There were five FBM subs of the *Ethan Allen* class, which began to enter service before the end of 1961. They were equipped from the start to handle an improved, 1,500-mile version of Polaris. Then came thirty-one ships in the *Lafayette* class. Each of those was barely 20 feet shorter than the mammoth *Triton* had been; and they were far heavier. Yet each of the new subs was powered by a single, advanced reactor, which produced an underwater speed of close to 30 knots. And each was built so that its missile tubes could be modified to carry larger rockets later on. New Polaris rocket casings were made of fiberglass instead of steel to save weight. These longer-range missiles were gradually fitted into both the old and new submarines. No place on earth is more than 2,000 miles from the sea; so every city or base in the world was then brought within the new 2,900-mile range of the missile subs.

In 1969 the Navy began to convert thirty-one of its

A Poseidon missile roars skyward in a test. Firing a missile of more than 32 tons produces a jolting change in a sub's weight and balance, but one of these ships returns to "trim" within seconds.

forty-one FBM submarines to carry the successor to Polaris—called Poseidon. By 1975 each of the sixteen missile tubes aboard each ship was supposed to contain a taller, fatter, more accurate ballistic rocket with twice the payload of the most advanced Polaris and a greater ability to get past enemy defenses. Each Poseidon weighs more than 32 tons and stands higher than a three-story building.

The latest development in U.S. missile subs is what was originally called "ULMS." Those letters stand for *U*ndersea *L*ong-range *M*issile *S*ystem, which will include a new series of subs with the code name *Trident*. Early in 1972 the U.S. Department of Defense announced plans to build the first of about twenty-five new subs before the end of the 1970's. Each *Trident* sub will be about half again as long as the old *Triton*, and its 15,000-ton displacement will dwarf any other underseas ship ever built. Each will have room for up to two dozen missiles. The first missiles will probably have the same diameter as Poseidon, so that they can be used in older subs, too; and their range is expected to be about 4,500 miles. Later, *Trident* subs will carry fatter, 6,000-mile missiles.

These new rockets will be so powerful that they could probably be modified to launch fair-sized earth satellites,

Trident *will be by far the largest submarine ever built. Eventually it will be armed with 6,000-mile-range ballistic missiles.*

but their announced purpose was to deliver H-bombs against any country that opened an all-out attack on the United States. The longer range means that such subs would never need to patrol in the area of a potential enemy. A *Trident* missile carrier could stay close to American shores, or it could have two-thirds of the earth's surface on which to hide—so as not to become a target for surprise attack itself.

The *Trident* submarines will probably be quieter, more comfortable for the crews, and even more reliable than any of the earlier missile ships. Their design will borrow some innovations developed for the other major category of U.S. Navy subs—the attack vessels.

Since completing the *Skipjack* class in 1961, the United States has built two more major types of attack submarine and started a third and a fourth series. Thirteen members of the *Permit** class are now on duty, and there are thirty-five in the *Sturgeon* class that followed. All are larger than *Skipjack*; but they use the same basic power plant, so they are no faster. They can dive deeper, however; and they have taken some lessons from *Tullibee*. Part of their additional weight comes from sonar equipment in the bow, and their machinery is mounted so as to cut down on noisy vibrations. Quieter reduction gears and other such changes increased the total weight of the propulsion machinery by about 20 percent. Operating at greater depths also made a heavier hull necessary.

Another way of reducing noise is to eliminate pumps from the reactor. This can be done by using the natural circulation reactor, which was mentioned in Chapter Two. A reactor like this is bigger and heavier, however,

---

* This group was originally called the *Thresher* class because that was the name of the first one to be commissioned. *Thresher* sank in the Atlantic during the spring of 1963, and the investigation and studies that followed that tragedy delayed the construction of additional U.S. subs briefly. The results are discussed in Chapter Six of this book.

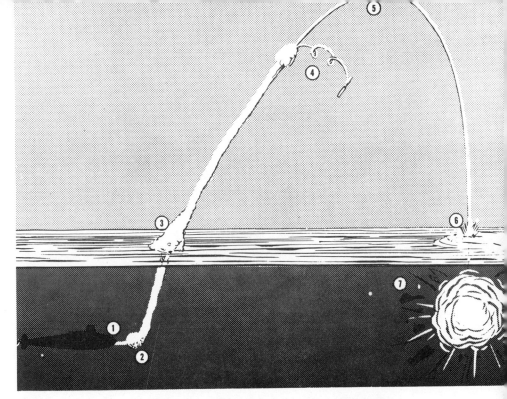

Sub vs. *sub: A submerged killer submarine (1) fires a SUBROC missile (2), which ignites its solid fuel while still under water and then breaks into the open (3). Shortly after the booster portion drops away (4), the two-ton nuclear warhead reaches the peak of its ballistic trajectory (5). The warhead arms itself as it crashes back through the waves (6), and explodes at the right depth to destroy an enemy (7) many miles from the launch point.*

so its use cuts a sub's speed still more. Each pound of extra equipment on a submarine adds three pounds to the ship's overall weight because of the extra ballast space required.

Modern attack subs are all better armed than earlier ones. Besides torpedoes, they may carry SUBROC missiies—weapons which can be fired at another ship (even an enemy submarine) while the attack sub remains underwater.

The next set of sweeping changes in U.S. nuclear sub design is going to come from two new programs—one to test a completely new electric-drive system on *Lipscomb*

Lipscomb *begins a new series of U.S. attack subs whose turbine-electric propulsion system will make them ultraquiet.*

(SSN 685), and the second to install more powerful propulsion equipment in future attack subs like *Los Angeles* (SSN 688) so that they can travel faster. Since subs of the *Los Angeles* class will be almost 70 feet longer and will weigh more than half again as much as *Sturgeon*, they may be able to take advantage of the quieter natural circulation reactor, too. This wouldn't make them as quiet as electric subs, but it might represent a good compromise between the ultimate in speed and the ultimate in silence. The *Los Angeles* class is supposed to be fast enough to keep up with (and help to protect) task forces on the surface, so these subs will probably be in the 35-knot range.

At present, U.S. officials admit that the Soviet Union has some submarines which are faster and some which are quieter than most of the American nukes. By the mid-1970's, advanced Russian nuclear subs carrying missiles will also outnumber our Navy's FBM's. Still, a comparison is difficult at any time because there are so many different types of nuclear subs in the Russian fleet.

The Russians probably didn't complete their first nuclear submarine until 1958, and it didn't go to sea immediately. But by 1961 they were boasting publicly that

78

they had "quite a few." This was a period when many Westerners were still skeptical about Russian technical claims, so they ignored announcements by the Soviet Union that its subs were faster than ours and could also carry atomic rockets. A couple of years later, the USSR released a photo of one of its subs, which the caption said had been taken among ice fields at the North Pole. It appeared to be about the same size as the attack subs being launched at that time by the United States, and its top deck was similarly rounded. This was one of the earliest Soviet nukes, however; and most of the subs in this "November"* class had probably been completed by the time the picture was published.

Early reports about Soviet nuclear subs indicated that they were bulkier and slower than those of the United States, even though their reactors might be a little more powerful. The "Echo" class was to carry missiles; but apparently they were air-breathers which could be fired only while a sub was on the surface. Their maximum range was assumed to be far short of the Regulus, which the U.S. Navy was ready to discard. Furthermore, winged cruise missiles take up a lot of room on a sub. Only half a dozen or so could be carried.

Early in 1966 two or three Russian nukes circled the earth while remaining submerged; and Soviet bloc officials began to talk more openly about a "blue belt" of missiles which covered all the oceans. Their "Hotel" class sub had launching tubes built into its sail for three large but short-ranged ballistic missiles. Although early versions could be launched only after surfacing, there was

---

* Different types of Russian submarines are designated by letters of the alphabet—"N," "E," "Y," etc. However, they are also known by the words which stand for these letters in the international alphabet. Thus, "November" means the same as "N" class. "Echo" means "E" class, "Yankee" means "Y" class, etc.

Four classes of Russian nuclear submarines: *(opposite top),* November, *(opposite bottom),* Hotel; *(above),* Charlie; *(below),* Yankee.

little reason to doubt that later models would be fired from beneath the surface.

Then, in 1968, the world's view of the Soviet nuclear fleet changed abruptly. Several new classes of Russian submarines appeared at once. The speed of the "Victor"-type attack submarine was reported at around 31 knots—which makes it extremely dangerous to other subs in a chase. The highly streamlined "Charlie" class (loaded with eight modern cruise missiles which can "home in" on targets 450 miles away) was suspected of being even faster because of its higher rated reactor. But the "Yankee" class was the biggest surprise of all. A Russian Y-type submarine looks like the American *Ethan Allen* class, but it is bigger than any FBM built by the United States so far and its speed is an impressive 29 knots. Each Yankee carries sixteen ballistic missiles, capable of being fired about 1,500 miles (2,400 kilometers). These SSN-6 missiles were shorter and slimmer than the ones first used by Russian subs, but their range was greater. It matched Polaris.

Y-class Soviet subs were spotted quickly in both the Atlantic and Pacific, patrolling both coasts of the United States. In addition to more than fifty other missile-launching nukes, the USSR will have more than forty "Yankees" by 1974. The hull of a Y-class submarine is only large enough to handle a dozen of the Russians' longer-ranged Sawfly missiles, however; so some successor to this submarine can be expected, too. Sawfly is roughly equivalent to Poseidon.

The "Papa" class of Russian nuclear submarine was kept secret until several years later. As a follow-on to the "Charlie" subs, it also carries cruise missiles. They are probably intended for use against ships, and it is difficult to guard against them because they can sneak in on their targets at fairly low altitudes. Furthermore, cruise missiles were not included in the first agreement between the

BALLISTIC MISSILES CARRIED BY SUBS

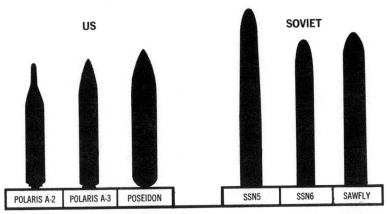

US				SOVIET		
POLARIS A-2	POLARIS A-3	POSEIDON		SSN5	SSN6	SAWFLY

The Soviet Union's sub missiles (at right) are bulkier than U.S. counterparts, but they lack the range of Poseidon. Better ones are being tested.

United States and the USSR to put limits on future submarine and rocket production.

With attack subs and all the older missile subs included, the Soviet Union has had a larger nuclear submarine fleet than the United States since 1971; and the Russians are unlikely to lose that lead any time soon. The Severodvinsk shipyard on the White Sea, for instance, can turn out about a dozen subs each year all by itself. By comparison, all of the shipyards in the United States have never completed more than thirteen nuclear subs in any one year. Even though the Russians seemed to be slowing down in 1971 and 1972, they were still building three or four times as many nukes as the United States.

It's true that the treaty to cut back on nuclear missile forces will have some effect. The Russians have agreed to scrap some of their older missile subs (diesels or nukes) as soon as new construction reaches a certain point. Nevertheless—counting all types—the nuclear submarine navy of the USSR will continue to edge ahead in numbers, if not in overall effectiveness, during the next few years. By 1975 the USSR should have more than one hundred and fifty nukes.

A British attack sub (above) and missile launcher (below). Note the whale-shaped bow.

There is also a possibility that the aircraft carrier being built now by the Russians will use nuclear propulsion. That would make it the first surface nuke warship in the world outside the U.S. Navy.

Meanwhile, the British and French are moving along more slowly, as late starters in the nuclear sub race. Between them, the two countries have completed an even dozen so far—with at least half a dozen more being built.

At about the time *Nautilus* was first displaying its versatility by a visit to the North Pole, the United States agreed to provide a reactor and propulsion equipment for the first British nuke, called *Dreadnought*. From the sail to the tail, this killer sub was almost a duplicate of *Skipjack*; but the British craft wasn't ready for duty until April, 1963. Naval architects in the United Kingdom designed a unique front end, which was to make their submarines look very much like whales. As in the case of the *Skipjack* hull, the idea is to increase underwater speed.

Since *Dreadnought*, the British have produced both the hulls and the propulsion systems for their nuclear subs. Their first attack subs after that were *Valiant* and *Warspite*, which were commissioned in 1966 and 1967. After a pause of several years, they continued the *Valiant* class with *Churchill*—which was completed in 1970.

There have been some improvements along the way, and these British subs match their U.S. counterparts closely. A new one is launched about every year, so the United Kingdom should have nine attack-type nuclear submarines by 1976.

The British also put four Polaris-carrying submarines into service during the latter part of the 1960's. Their names are *Resolution, Repulse, Renown*, and *Revenge*. Each carries sixteen Polaris missiles, and each ship is a bit larger than an American FBM-type. Displacement at the surface is about 7,500 tons.

Finally, there are French subs. On March 29, 1967,

Two views of a French missile-firing nuclear submarine.

President Charles de Gaulle applauded proudly as the 7,900-ton *Redoutable* slid down the launching ramp at Cherbourg. It was the first ship in his nation's nuclear navy. Only a few months later, the keel was laid for a sister ship, *Terrible. Foudroyant* and *Indomptable* followed at two-year intervals.

They are French ships in every detail. The reactors use uranium enriched by the French themselves. The sixteen missile tubes on each will be armed with a French version of Polaris—tipped with a 500-kiloton nuclear warhead developed exclusively by that country. These are probably the slowest of the world's nuclear FBM subs. Still, they represent a mighty striking force.

It is no coincidence that each of the French subs carries sixteen missiles, the same number found on U.S. subs, British subs, and the first Yankee-class Russian subs. Balancing weights and volumes is terribly important in designing a submarine. If you start with roughly the same sized missile and power plant, the best layout usually includes two rows of eight missiles each. As missiles, power plants, and submarine hulls grow larger, of course, a different number and different arrangement may prove better.

France had started out in the 1950's to build a nuclear attack sub, but later canceled the project. There was also a time when the French Navy seemed ready to order nuclear propulsion for surface ships. Except for the possibility that the Russians might be building a nuclear aircraft carrier, however, the United States Navy still has no challengers in this respect.

Chapter Three explained the advantages of nuclear-powered aircraft carriers, so it should be easy to understand why the U.S. Navy's nuclear fleet is planned around carriers. *Enterprise* has been in action since 1961, steaming well over half a million miles while taking on only two new loads of fuel. The second nuclear air-

Truxtun *(above) and* California *(opp.)—two missile-armed frigates.*

craft carrier, *Nimitz,* was launched in 1972; and construction is well under way on a third—*Eisenhower.* The fourth was approved by Congress in 1972, but it is not expected to be ready for service until the early 1980's.

Design of the first nuclear carrier started in 1950, the same year *Nautilus* was authorized. The much more costly surface ship project was delayed and interrupted, however; and the actual contract to build *Enterprise* wasn't awarded until November 15, 1957. The first big step in construction (the laying of the keel) took place on February 4, 1958. The ship was christened and launched nineteen months later, and the first of its eight reactors began test operations less than six weeks after that. After brief sea trials, *Enterprise* formally joined the fleet by being commissioned on November 25, 1961.

It is customary for a carrier to lead its own task force. Only nuclear-powered ships can move at the pace set by the U.S. nuclear carriers, so eventually half a dozen or more nuclear frigates will join them. The first two were *Bainbridge* and *Truxtun*, commissioned in 1962 and 1967 respectively. Next came *California* and *South Carolina*, entering service in the early 1970's. The slightly larger *Virginia* and two others are scheduled to be ready some time after 1975, when *Eisenhower* is slated to be commissioned.

The only other surface warship to use nuclear propulsion so far is the cruiser *Long Beach*, which began service shortly before *Enterprise*. It was the first cruiser built by

A Terrier missile charges from the foredeck of Long Beach.

the United States after World War II, and it could well be the last. *Long Beach* was planned originally as a 7,800-ton destroyer, but designers kept adding new weapons and electronic systems until they turned it into a vessel that displaces more than 17,000 tons. Ships of this type require a crew of about 1,000—nearly twice as many as a nuclear frigate; and they cost a lot more because they are so big. Nowadays, a missile-equipped frigate half this size can do approximately the same job.

All of the surface ships built as escorts for American nuclear carriers are heavily armed. *Bainbridge,* for instance, carries two batteries of supersonic missiles to protect it against aerial attack. There are also six torpedo tubes amidships. The ASROC (antisubmarine rocket) system can launch either target-seeking torpedoes or nuclear depth charges against a threatening submarine. Of course, the ships in a nuclear carrier task force are also shielded by the umbrella of aircraft which can rise quickly from the vast decks of the carrier itself.

The dimensions of a nuclear aircraft carrier are awesome: Compared to a well-known landmark like the U.S. Capitol, the carrier is considerably longer. Its flight deck is nearly as wide. The top of its mast would fall just short of the statue atop the Capitol's dome. *Enterprise* weighs in at 89,400 tons, and its successors will displace about 95,000 tons each when fully equipped for combat. Yet these monstrous vessels roar through the water tirelessly

"The sub that sailed in the desert." The world's first power-producing nuclear reactor was operated inside the horizontal hull section shown here inside a four-story-high water tank at Arco, Idaho. A duplicate went into Nautilus.

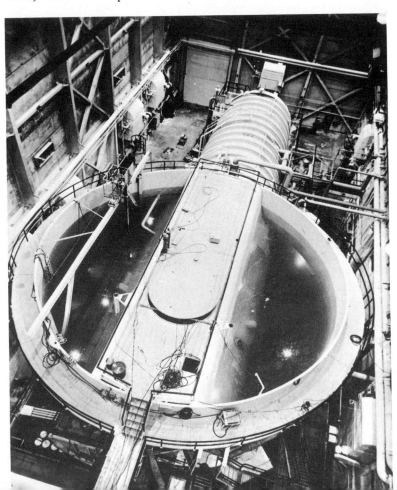

at 35 knots. And their new long-life reactor cores will last for ten to thirteen years before a fuel change is necessary.

Nimitz and *Eisenhower* will each use only two powerful reactors instead of the eight smaller nuclear plants aboard *Enterprise*. There are two reactors on each of the smaller surface ships in the U.S. Navy, too. Each of the reactors on the smaller ships produces about as much power as the older ones on *Enterprise*—enough from each reactor to provide 35,000 shaft horsepower of propulsive energy. That means that they have more driving force than the ones being used now on American submarines; so it might be possible to adapt the surface-ship reactors to fit into the powerful new submarines which the Navy is building now. On the other hand, it might be better just to add a second reactor to each sub—as *Triton* did. There are other ways in which the speed of nuclear ships could be increased too, but those will be covered in Chapter Nine.

Before a completely new type of reactor is installed in any U.S. Navy ship, a full-sized prototype is tested on land. In the case of both *Nautilus* and *Enterprise*, the land-based reactors were actually fitted into simulated hull structures and connected to steam generators and propulsion machinery. The submarine hull was even inserted into a tank of water. More than eighteen months before *Nautilus* put out to sea, a Navy crew had completed a full-power submerged "crossing" of the Atlantic Ocean—right in the midst of a southeastern Idaho desert.

Such attention to practical detail has been vital. It's one reason that nuclear naval ships have been so successful. The push to produce commercial nukes has never been a life-or-death matter, however. It's natural that they have developed more slowly.

CHAPTER FIVE

The Peaceful Ones

There are almost as many differences as similarities among the handful of peaceful nuclear ships which now exist. Those built so far were built for varied reasons, and the ones being planned will add more variety. Nevertheless, it's possible (and probably helpful) to divide peaceful nukes into three broad groups: (1) surface ships used to deliver people or goods; (2) surface ships with special tasks, like icebreaking; and (3) submersibles—either to carry cargo or to do research. The first group is the largest, and it will probably be the most important for many years. It's a logical starting place, and most of this chapter will be devoted to it.

Nuclear merchantmen now being planned by the United States, Japan, and the Federal Republic of Germany are many times as powerful as the old museum piece, N.S. *Savannah*. Yet they all trace their history to that vessel. No matter how much money had been spent on research and development, it was inevitable that someone would eventually take the costly step of building the first commercial nuclear ship. Operating it would be part of the development process. The United States decided to take the step quickly, and that's how *Savannah* was born. The ship's brief life was generally a successful

N.S. Savannah's *major assignment was to show the world that nuclear propulsion could be applied to a commercial-type ship. Savannah was plush and pretty but not well designed as a cargo carrier.*

one, but it also had its share of misunderstanding and misfortune.

At first, things went smoothly. Less than seven months after *Nautilus*—the first nuclear ship of any sort— entered service, President Dwight D. Eisenhower proposed another kind of ship to demonstrate the *peaceful* possibilities of atomic energy. During the following year (1956), Congress authorized N.S. *Savannah**; and by the spring of 1957 a contract for the ship's construction was awarded. The keel laying early in 1958 and launching on July 21, 1959, were colorful events. In the first instance, Mrs. Richard M. Nixon (whose husband was then Vice

---

* The letters stand for "Nuclear Ship"—a designation corresponding to that of "S.S." (Steam Ship), "M.S." (Motor Ship), or "G.T.S" (Gas Turbine Ship).

President) did the honors with an "atomic wand." This was a small rod containing a bit of radioactive material, symbolizing the new Age of the Peaceful Atom. As Mrs. Nixon brought the wand near a Geiger counter, that instrument clicked out its radiation reading and the sounds were amplified as a signal to a crane operator. That was the dramatic cue for the workman to swing the first giant keel section into place.

Construction took longer than planned, but by the spring of 1961 work was practically complete on what some marine engineers still consider the most beautiful ship ever built. *Savannah* was white and sleek. It needed no smokestacks, of course; and its superstructure slanted back to give it the look of a racer. It was about the size of a *Mariner*-class cargo ship—not quite 600 feet long, with a displacement of some 21,800 tons. As a demonstration vessel, however, Savannah was outfitted handsomely to carry sixty passengers as well as cargo. Public safety hearings led to a go-ahead in the summer of 1961 for fueling and start-up.

Savannah's nuclear fuel was loaded into its reactor with remarkable speed. It took less than thirty hours to insert all thirty-two fuel bundles, which would propel the historic ship on the equivalent of more than thirteen trips around the world. During her sea trials, the captain also showed that *Savannah*'s reactor could actually surpass its original objectives. Instead of delivering 20,000 shaft horsepower to the single propeller, the power plant easily produced more than 22,300. Instead of being limited to about 20 knots, *Savannah* surged along at 24. And it looked as if top speed might be as high as 27 knots.

Unlike the nuclear warships, nothing about *Savannah* was secret. Instead of copying a Navy reactor, its developers had produced a brand-new power plant design—using cheaper, low enriched uranium. Details of the vessel's propulsion system were published all over the world. Besides giving reactor builders and naval architects some practical data with which they could refine future models, *Savannah* even showed off to the crowds at the 1962 Seattle World's Fair. Visitors streamed through a viewing gallery that let them look right down into the glass-enclosed control room. Several countries announced that they too would soon be building nuclear merchant ships. The pressurized-water power plant aboard *Savannah* functioned beautifully.

Then, suddenly, the triumphal cruises were interrupted by an argument over salaries!

Engineering officers on *Savannah* had been granted extra pay from the outset, because they needed nuclear know-how in addition to their other qualifications and because their training period had lasted longer than anyone had expected. However, the union of officers on deck insisted that they should still be paid *more* than the engineers—because a deck officer's duties were traditionally more demanding. An arbitrator agreed with the deck officers, but the engineers refused to accept the ruling. On May 6, 1963—just before *Savannah* was to leave Galveston, Texas—the engineers shut down the ship's reactor in protest. Three days later, they turned off the *Savannah*'s water. Finally, the striking engineers even disconnected the power lines coming onto the ship from shore. Through no fault of her own, *Savannah* was temporarily paralyzed.

Nobody could persuade the engineers to go back to work so long as they were being paid less than the deck officers. In desperation, the Federal Maritime Administration finally canceled its contract with the shipping line it had chosen to operate *Savannah*. A new line was picked, but this meant that an entirely new crew (from a different union) would have to be recruited and trained.

For almost a year, the world's first nuclear merchant

ship sat at its dock—in perfect shape, but going nowhere. It didn't seem to matter *why* the voyages had stopped; *Savannah*'s prestige crumbled. The American public was embarrassed and annoyed that such an expensive and well-publicized product was unable to perform.

When the new crew was ready at last, *Savannah* steamed back into the spotlight; and again she was a star. More than 150,000 men, women, and children clambered aboard her at the first four European ports she visited. They couldn't help but be impressed by her spotless corridors and plush furnishings. These even included paintings and sculpture on loan from the Whitney Museum of American Art in New York City.

Most people failed to realize, however, that *Savannah* had never been expected to operate at a profit. It started out with a crew of one hundred and ten—ridiculously large for a commercial cargo ship. Placement of the superstructure and masts made the vessel pretty to look at, but it also made one of the holds unusually difficult to load. The angle also exaggerated the fact that *Savannah*'s crane was too light. *Savannah* was a showhorse, not a workhorse, and she had never been intended to be anything different.

The hope had been that *Savannah* would be followed rather quickly by other commercial nukes. They would be bigger, of course, in order to emphasize the cost savings in fuel. It also seemed logical to assume that both their propulsion units and their hull designs could be improved over those of *Savannah*. After all, the chief goal on the demonstration ship had simply been to make sure everything worked. Yet all the opportunities for improvement led to a strange standstill. The Atomic Energy Commission was inclined to concentrate on developing the best possible propulsion system, while the Federal Maritime Administration showed more interest in developing an optimum ship design. Which should come first?

If the engineers' strike had not stalled things for a while—and *if* the stepped-up war in Vietnam during the mid-1960's had not begun to squeeze the federal budget —*both* developments might have been pushed. Instead, however, *Savannah* was to remain the only nuclear merchant ship flying the U.S. flag for more than a decade. And people became more and more impatient with the fact that *Savannah* couldn't be transformed into something she had never pretended to be.

In mid-1965, the AEC issued a license to First Atomic Ship Transport, Inc., to operate *Savannah* commercially for three years. The company had been formed as a subsidiary of American Export Isbrandtsen Lines just for this purpose; and the line was charged no rent on the vessel in order to help make up for the higher cost of operating a demonstration ship. The luxurious cabins were stripped out, and the passenger spaces were sealed off. About 1,800 tons of solid ballast were removed, and *Savannah* left New York on September 3, 1965, for the first time with a capacity load of 10,000 tons of general cargo. The crew was reduced to around seventy, but that was still far more than on a conventional freighter of the

Only one fuel stop was needed during Savannah's *lifetime, and then most of the fuel bundles were simply shuffled around to make them "burn up" more evenly.*

same class. *Savannah*'s power plant equipment was so spread out that a larger engine crew than normal would always be needed. Strict safety regulations required health physics specialists aboard, and extra deck officers were kept on duty at all times—even when the ship was in port. There was never any real hope of making *Savannah* pay its own way, although its losses each year were not great.

Even in her new role, *Savannah* continued to serve as a goodwill ambassador and a cruising exhibit for peaceful use of the atom. She visited Africa and the Far East. In the fall of 1968, N.S. *Savannah* spent about two months at a Galveston shipyard for refueling and maintenance, but the servicing crew beat its original schedule by a full week and the U.S.A.'s nuclear merchantman was back in operation early.

Actually, the refueling itself took only two weeks. Even after nearly 350,000 miles, only four of the thirty-two fuel bundles had to be replaced. These were the ones at the center of the reactor, where the fissioning action takes place most vigorously. The other bundles were merely rearranged so that the core would release energy more evenly again.

A second complete core was built for *Savannah*, but it was never installed. Even though the board chairman of American Export Isbrandtsen Lines called her "the most reliable ship we have operating," the U.S. Maritime Administration decided that little more could be gained from the $90,000,000-plus which had been invested in the entire *Savannah* project. A last-minute suggestion to let the Army use her as a floating power plant in emergencies came too late. In the fall of 1971 the glamorous queen of the peaceful nukes headed into retirement.

Many lessons learned from *Savannah* helped to make West Germany's N.S. *Otto Hahn* a more effective ship.

Hahn's small nuclear steam source is only about half as powerful as *Savannah*'s, but its design will save an enormous amount of space and weight when it is copied on a larger scale. The basic design of the German reactor was created by the same U.S. company which had worked on the one for *Savannah* (Babcock & Wilcox); but *Otto Hahn* had two advantages. It was built later and on a much slower schedule.

A shipyard at Kiel (in northern Germany) was given the contract to build *Otto Hahn* in 1962—the year in which *Savannah* was attracting throngs of visitors at the Seattle World's Fair. The keel was laid in the following year, and the hull was launched in mid-1964; but *Hahn* was not finished until 1968. By that time, some people in the United States thought *Savannah* had already outlived her usefulness.

Hahn is in part a research ship. In addition to a crew of more than seventy, she carries between thirty and thirty-five engineers and scientists who use complicated electrical and electronic instruments to study every phase of the ship's performance. But basically this is a working vessel. N.S. *Otto Hahn* hauls ore, and it does the job well. It has traveled to tropical ports and to the Far North, covering nearly 200,000 miles before its first refueling in 1972.

German authorities had considered building a nuclear tanker or a passenger ship, but they decided on an ore carrier for many reasons. First of all, ore carriers are simple ships; this would keep costs down. They could also save money by making their first nuclear vessel a small one; but the power plant and propulsion machinery would have to occupy a certain minimum space. If *Hahn* were designed to carry a *dense* cargo (like ore), it would be possible to squeeze a respectably heavy payload into a small volume. Finally, there is very little fire hazard aboard an ore ship, and its stubby shape can be used to

Carrying ore isn't a glamorous job, but N.S. Otto Hahn *does it well. The Germans chose this type of ship because it is simple, cheap, safe, and reasonably useful.*

make it practically unsinkable. To the extent that nuclear propulsion was still experimental, this would be an extraordinarily safe way to experiment.

Otto Hahn is almost exactly the same length as *Savannah*, and when the German ship is empty it weighs slightly less. But *Hahn*'s cargo weight is roughly half again as much as *Savannah*'s. When the ship is fully loaded with 14,000 tons of ore, *Hahn*'s less powerful reactor produces a top speed of about 17 knots.

It is only a coincidence; but the reactor fuel core aboard squat little *Hahn* is rather squat, too. Its bundles of pellet-filled tubes are shorter and fatter than those used by *Savannah*—although there are only half as many separate bundles in the German core.

The most striking difference in the design of *Hahn*'s power plant, however, is the fact that there are no big steam generator tanks outside the reactor's pressure vessel—no bulky connecting pipes. (See figure page 104). Heat is transferred from the reactor coolant water to a separate water supply right inside the same pressure-tight container. That saves weight, and reduces the chance of coolant leaks, too.

Japan's first nuclear ship, *Mutsu*, is a lot less sophisticated than either its U.S. or its German predecessor. *Mutsu* is only 130 meters (about 428 feet) in overall length, and displaces just 10,400 tons. The Japanese vessel is classified as a "special cargo" ship, but the three holds can carry only 2,400 tons.

Like those on *Savannah* and *Hahn*, the reactor chosen for *Mutsu* is a pressurized-water type using uranium oxide fuel of between 4 percent and 5 percent enrichment. Its power output nearly matches the German reactor, but the propulsion system on *Mutsu* provides slightly less horsepower to the propeller shaft. Top speed for *Hahn* and *Mutsu* is about the same, despite the fact that the Japanese ship is so much smaller and lighter.

Back in 1963 the newly established Japan Nuclear Ship Development Agency had hoped for bigger things. There was talk of large nuclear-powered freighters, of a cargo-carrying submarine, and, finally, of an oceanographic research ship. Costs at that time were too high, however; and in 1967 the agency decided to start with the less ambitious *Mutsu* project. Except for the slightly enriched fuel material (which came from the United States) and a few components supplied by manufacturers in the United States and West Germany, *Mutsu* was a home-grown product. Everything else was produced in Japan, although the reactor had actually been designed in the United States by Westinghouse. The keel was laid at Tokyo Shipyard near the end of 1968, and the hull was launched less than seven months later. Sea trials with a nonnuclear propulsion system were completed in 1971, but the delivery of the reactor itself was delayed until the following year.

Mutsu has a crew of between fifty-five and sixty, and there are also twenty researchers aboard to use the ship as a floating nuclear laboratory. Because of the small cargo capacity and the specialized training of the crew, one idea is to use *Mutsu* in transporting radioactive waste materials and spent fuel elements from Japan's rapidly growing nuclear power industry. Such items are not very big or heavy, but, obviously, they require expert handling.

Above all, *Mutsu* is a school. It will help to train crews for a fleet of three hundred nuclear container ships which Japanese nuclear authorities now predict will be built during the last twenty years of this century. Ordinarily, a forecast like this might not be believable. After all, the original worldwide optimism about nuclear ships which *Savannah* generated led to disappointment in most cases. Yet this new projection *is* different. In May, 1971, Japan and the Federal Republic of Germany announced defi-

Mutsu *represented the first small step for Japan in the field of nuclear propulsion.*

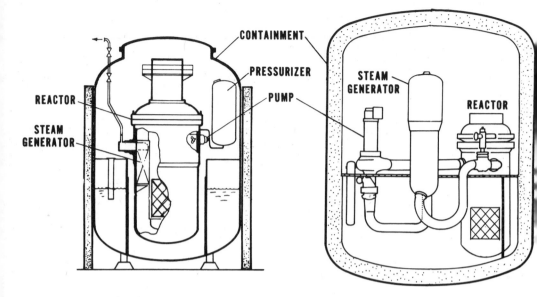

CONTAINMENT
PRESSURIZER
PUMP
REACTOR
STEAM GENERATOR
STEAM GENERATOR
REACTOR

A highly simplified comparison of two nuclear steam-source designs for approximately the same power level shows the advantage of the newer system on the left. The "spread out" arrangement at right requires a bigger and heavier containment shell. By putting the steam generators right alongside the reactor core (cross-hatched area), inside *a slightly enlarged vessel, advanced nukes save space and weight.*

nite plans to cooperate in building two nuclear cargo ships which should be large enough and fast enough to pay their own way in carrying containers of cargo back and forth between the two countries. Each will have 80,000 shaft horsepower—eight times the propulsive force of little *Mutsu* and nearly four times that of N.S. *Savannah*. The nuclear power plants will be German-built advanced pressurized-water systems like the one on *Otto Hahn*, so they will probably weigh no more than *Savannah's*. The ships themselves will be designed in Japan.

The United States—the country that started it all—does not expect to be left behind in the new spurt to build nuclear merchant ships. After careful economic and engineering studies, the U.S. Maritime Administration proposed that this country begin work sometime during 1974 on three cargo ships which would be even more powerful than the ones planned jointly by Germany and Japan. The new American nukes are to use pressurized-water reactors, and each ship in the trio is expected to develop 120,000 shaft horsepower. The idea of producing three ships of the same type is to cut the cost of each one. It is almost always cheaper to make several copies of the same piece of equipment than it would be to design and manufacture each one individually. For the same reason, fuel elements for new nuclear ships will probably be very similar (except in length) to the ones already being manufactured on a production-line basis for land reactors.

It is difficult to estimate exactly how long it will take now before other nations follow the lead of the United States, Germany, and Japan in building commercial nuclear ships. Italy could probably do so by the beginning of the 1980's, but its nuclear ship project has been delayed repeatedly by one problem or another. The Italians plan a ship to be called N.S. *Enrico Fermi*, but no definite date has been scheduled for it to be ready for operation. Late in 1966 *Fermi* became a joint project of the Italian Navy (commissioned to design the vessel) and Italy's National Commission for Atomic Energy (responsible for nuclear aspects). The aim was to have about 90 percent of the work on *Fermi* done in Italy, but problems arose because Italy has no means of enriching uranium. Even though *Fermi* would not be a warship, it was to be operated by the Italian Navy. That meant that the United States couldn't supply enriched uranium for its reactor without a special act of Congress, and this couldn't be arranged. The French declined to supply it either. So the Italians decided to reorganize the program, making it clear that *Fermi* is only intended to be a peaceful nuke. The exact nature of the ship would be up to the shipping company with which the Italian government came to terms.

Italy's first nuclear ship may well be a small tanker, but it will also be used for crew training. *Fermi*'s original design called for a vessel comparable in size and power to *Savannah*, but a bit lighter—with a displacement of 18,000 tons. The ship was supposed to accommodate 350 men (mostly trainees) and carry about 9,300 tons of cargo. At that size, obviously, it could not be an economic

Giant ships like these could be next on the schedule for the United States in the field of peaceful nukes. (Cutaways show location of nuclear power sources.)

success; but it was supposed to open the way for larger ships later on. Now the Italians may insist on a bigger vessel immediately in order to make it a moneymaker from the start.

France, Belgium, the Netherlands, Norway, Sweden, and the United Kingdom all seemed ready during the early 1960's to produce commercial nuclear ships of some sort—either tankers or freighters. Reactor designs were drawn, and land tests were conducted with some components. Euratom, an agency in which a number of Western European nations cooperate, helped to finance some of the projects. One by one, however, each country came to a conclusion which the British stated most forcefully: They were unwilling to invest in actually *building* a nuclear merchant ship until it was clear that such ships could produce some profit. Rising costs of fuel oil and the increasing need for large, fast, powerful ships will finally satisfy that condition during the late 1970's. If all these countries keep their word, the Great White Fleet of peaceful nukes should expand suddenly during the next decade.

The People's Republic of China is in a slightly different position. French journalists reported in 1962 that the Chinese Nuclear Energy Commission and the Ministry of Transport on the mainland had begun to develop a nuclear ship with the help of the Soviet Union. A couple of years later, the keel was supposed to have been laid for a nuclear ship called *Zan Than* ("Voice of the People"). According to one account, it intended to use a reactor more than twice as powerful as *Savannah*'s, fueled with slightly enriched uranium dioxide. It was expected to be about the same size as the U.S. ship, and a little faster.

It seems now that if construction ever really began on *Zan Than* (or its successor, *Bac Phan*) there has been a long delay in completing it. China lost the help of Rus-

The growing merchant fleet of the People's Republic of China is symbolized by this oil tanker completed in 1970. The country seems likely to launch a nuclear ship soon, if only for prestige.

sian technicians when the two countries began to quarrel openly over interpretations of Communist philosophy. Power struggles within China upset many national plans. Now that the People's Republic of China has joined the United Nations and has begun to increase its associations with other countries, however, it's clear that it is only a matter of time before the old nuclear ship projects there are revived or new ones are launched. Chinese prestige would be boosted all over the world by its own reactor-driven cargo vessel—whether the ship made economic sense or not.

Aside from merchant vessels, the only peaceful nukes which are likely to operate in the near future are ice-breakers and submarines. The USSR seems to hold a monopoly in the first category, and the United States has a similar position in regard to the second.

The Soviet Union's *Lenin* was actually the first non-military vessel to be propelled by nuclear power. The 16,000-ton-displacement icebreaker was launched on December 5, 1957, and put into service two years later. *Lenin* was out of commission between 1966 and 1969, while its original three pressurized-water reactors were replaced by two more powerful ones; but apparently the Russians are pleased with the idea of nuclear icebreakers. At least two more are nearing completion. They are being built in Finnish shipyards for the Soviet Union, and they should be operating by the mid-1970's.

Lenin is quite different from any of the cargo-carrying nukes. It does an excellent job at its own special task, however, because the vessel was designed especially for it. An icebreaker needs lots of power; *Lenin* can produce up to 44,000 shaft horsepower from its pressurized-water reactors. An icebreaker should be fairly short in comparison to its width; this enables her to turn in a limited space and to cut a broad path in the ice when she operates. Although *Lenin* is one and a half times as wide as *Mutsu*, the Russian ship is only a few feet longer. Above all, an ideal icebreaker should have endurance. The ship should be able to work at full power around the clock, operating at great distances from her home base without needing to return for fuel frequently or to depend on a vulnerable support ship to tag along with her. A nuclear icebreaker like *Lenin*, of course, can operate for more than a year at a time on its own if necessary. *Lenin* carries a crew of close to one thousand men. There are shops aboard for minor repairs. It's said that even if one of the ship's three propellers were to break (a problem that isn't too unusual for an icebreaker in heavy pack ice) it could be replaced at sea.

Lenin's nuclear fuel is uranium oxide, enriched to the point where it is about 5 percent U-235. Instead of using the steam-driven turbines to spin the ship's propellers directly, the Russians use turbogenerators to produce electricity and then feed this power into electric motors

Russia's **Lenin** *icebreaker (above) carries a crew of about one thousand. Its captain has claimed it could crush its way through the ice pack all the way to the North Pole. The new* Arktika *(below) will be even larger.*

which turn the three propeller shafts. This is the same method used in the United States' new "quiet submarines," which were described earlier in this book. In *Lenin*'s case, however, the goal isn't to eliminate noise. Icebreakers have to start and stop a lot, and "electric drive" works better than a direct gear arrangement under those conditions.

Especially in the case of very thick pack ice, an icebreaker doesn't simply steam straight ahead. Its forward-slanting bow allows the chunky vessel to ride far up onto the edge of an ice sheet, where sheer weight causes the ship to come crunching down through it. Having bitten off one piece of the pack in this manner, the icebreaker backs up and roars forward at full power again. It means slow going and a bumpy ride.

In open water, *Lenin*'s top speed is about 18 knots; but clearly its forward progress is much slower through the ice. The ship manages to move through ice several yards thick, however; and *Lenin* has helped to lengthen the period during which ships can operate in the Russian Arctic from about ninety days a year to more than five months annually. If necessary, *Lenin*'s reactors can also heat water, which weakens the ice ahead of the ship when it is sprayed out in jets. Russian officials have boasted that *Lenin* could actually smash its way through all the way to the North Pole—except that they say the icebreaker is too important to spare on a voyage like that, even for the sake of setting a new record.

The Russian government adopted a resolution in 1964 to construct additional nuclear icebreakers, but the technical problems with *Lenin* which led to the replacement of its reactors may have caused a slowdown in the program. Articles in the Russian press have indicated that the next version will be longer and heavier than *Lenin*, displacing about 25,000 tons. Each is expected to have

111

two reactors, and the first new vessel has been given the name *Arktika*.

In 1970, however, the Russian newspaper *Izvestia* described plans for a couple of icebreaking nukes which would be even bigger and more powerful. That article said that they would be built in Leningrad and that each would be twice as powerful as *Lenin*—apparently giving each one more than 80,000 shaft horsepower. The new vessels are supposed to be equipped with as many as ten helicopters each, but it is hard to understand why so many helicopters would be needed for making ordinary ice surveys. If these ships are built (in addition to the ones under construction in Finland for the USSR), they may have some military role. For instance, they might work in

Humble's huge icebreaking tanker, S.S. Manhattan, had trouble in the Northwest Passage to Alaska. The 1,005-foot ship was nine times as heavy as Lenin, but it had less power. It may be followed by nukes that could do the job more easily.

conjunction with Russian nuclear submarines, which have been operating regularly under the Arctic ice for many years.

All seagoing U.S. icebreakers are now controlled by the Coast Guard, which has been interested for years in a big new nuke which could match or surpass *Lenin*'s performance. However, icebreakers are not considered as important to the United States as they are to the Soviet Union, which needs them to keep northern ports open. Rather than invest in a new and special type of nuclear surface ship, the Department of Defense decided to order several new conventionally fueled icebreakers during the 1970's. They will all be smaller than *Lenin*, yet each will be more powerful. Because their power will come from gas turbines instead of nuclear reactors, however, their range will be quite limited in comparison.

Voyages to Alaska by the specially modified oil tanker S.S. *Manhattan* point to another use of nuclear propulsion in the Far North. Instead of restricting commercial voyages to the channels opened by icebreaker escorts, cargo ships might be built with the proper type of bow and extra-strength hull to make such trips on their own. *Manhattan* had troubles because her 43,000 shp engines weren't really powerful enough for the task. If they had been large enough, however, there still would have been a big difficulty. They would have required so much fuel oil that hardly any cargo could have been carried on the return trip. Nuclear reactors could solve these problems. Some day, perhaps, they will.

Another way of transporting sea cargo in the Arctic, of course, would be to go *under* the ice. That possibility was mentioned earlier, and it will be considered more fully in the final chapter. At present, however, there is only one submersible nuke in the world which is not a warship; and it is far too small to haul either peaceful cargo *or*

113

weapons. It is the U.S. Navy's oceanographic research vehicle, *NR-1*.

NR-1 is a real midget in the world's nuclear fleet. The sub is only 140 feet long and 12 feet in diameter, and its entire crew consists of only seven men (including two scientific observers). It is also one of the few submarines ever built with *wheels*. Once it reaches the sea bottom, *NR-1* rolls along from place to place—making maps, recording temperatures and currents, and inspecting ocean life. The little sub's displacement is less than 400 tons—one-tenth the weight of *Nautilus*.

The men aboard *NR-1* can look out through three viewing ports near the front of the sub, using high-powered lights to slice through the dark waters. Movie and TV cameras are carried on the air-conditioned vessel, which has a small laboratory aboard, too. A mechanical arm can also reach out to pick things up off the bottom. This can be useful in examining sunken ships, in prospecting for minerals, or in rescue operations.

NR-1 can probably reach a depth of about 3,500 feet safely. Some other devices can carry men deeper, but none is as roomy as *NR-1* and none of the conventional deep-divers can move about as easily or stay down very long. *NR-1*'s only limit is the amount of food it can take along for its crew—about a thirty-day supply.

The water pressure at such great depths is enormous. Thick, heavy plates are needed to keep a vessel's walls from caving in under the strain; and this normally leaves little room for anything else. Many deep-diving submersibles are generally content just to go up and down over one spot by adjusting ballast; they cannot move about at a speed of more than two or three knots. *NR-1* is twice that fast, and it is quite maneuverable. Its twin propellers make it as much of an improvement over most submarine study craft as modern airplanes are over dirigibles.

The only nuclear submarine which is not a warship is NR-1—a small, deep-diving research vessel of the U.S. Navy.

The next nuclear-powered research sub exists only on paper so far, but Admiral Rickover told the Senate Appropriations Committee in 1971 what it would be like. By using a new type of steel, he explained, *NR-2* will be able to dive even deeper. With an improved reactor, it could be faster, too.

NR-1 was launched on January 25, 1961. Sea trials were completed during August that same year. Although it is fundamentally a peaceful nuke, *NR-1* carries out military studies. For that reason, the U.S. Navy has released very little information about the ship's design or about its small pressurized-water reactor. If a commercial firm should want to build a nuclear research sub on its own, it probably would not be free to borrow many ideas from the highly classified *NR-1*.

As a matter of fact, there has been relatively little cooperation between military and nonmilitary nuclear ship programs at all. Admiral Rickover has insisted that the problems faced by the two are quite different. As pointed out earlier, the costs have not been comparable either. Little *NR-1* cost about $100,000,000 to develop and build—more than was spent on the whole *Savannah* program from start to finish. At some point in the future, military and peaceful applications of nuclear ship propulsion may tend to merge, but that time probably is still a long way off.

CHAPTER SIX

How Safe?

Nuclear energy has been used peacefully (and safely) for more than a quarter of a century. As a tool for medical diagnosis and treatment, it literally saves lives every day, and it helps millions of people to live more comfortably. Yet the world still has not forgotten that the *first* use of nuclear energy was to kill and destroy. As a result, the question of nuclear hazards always comes up—about a shipboard reactor or any other device that taps the enormous power inside the atom.

This timid and skeptical attitude annoys many engineers. They think most popular fears are silly. They know that a propulsion reactor cannot explode like an A-bomb and that there is no reason to fear the tiny amount of radiation that can be detected in the passenger and work areas of a nuclear ship. Hopefully, the general public will eventually learn enough about the fundamentals of nuclear energy to distinguish between *real* hazards (which *can* exist, of course) and imaginary ones. Meanwhile, we shouldn't overlook the fact that the unusual public caution about nuclear systems has had some good effects.

From the start, industry had to stress safety in the design and construction and operation of nuclear reactors.

117

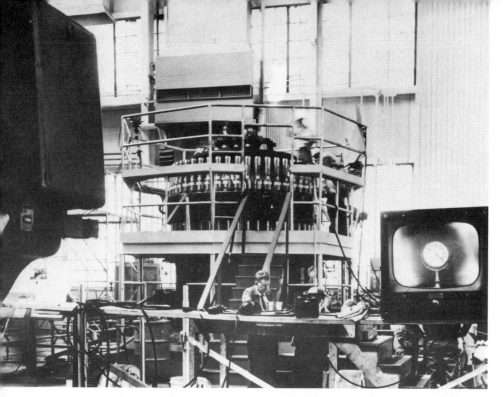

Nuclear ship safety begins with careful testing of every component. This reactor vessel had to go through more than 2,500 trials and inspections before it was installed.

Special regulations were drawn up in this country and around the world to eliminate possible dangers from radiation before they even had a chance to arise. As a result, nuclear technology developed more slowly but more surely. Nuclear ships—like power reactors on land —have compiled a fabulously good safety record. That contrasts with the first years of the steamboat—when boiler explosions were common and numerous ships and lives were lost. Many people doubted then that it would *ever* be considered safe to ride on a vessel propelled by a snorting, unpredictable steam engine. If the early history of *nuclear* ships had been anything like *that*, the whole idea would have been scrapped promptly.

The details of safety measures vary from one nuclear vessel to the next, but three basic objectives stay the same. The first is to make sure that the normal operation of the nuclear reactors doesn't endanger the crews, the passengers, or any people or places in the vicinity. The second is to make a nuclear ship itself as safe as (or safer than) a conventional vessel of the same type in meeting the usual perils of the sea. The final objective is to prevent any dangerous release of radioactivity in case such a ship *is* involved in some sort of accident—a collision, grounding, fire, explosions, flooding, or even sinking. Each of these three objectives represents a story in itself; so they might as well be considered separately, in that order.

As Chapter Two explained, there are always several distinct layers of shielding around the core of a ship reactor. They may include lead, steel, water, concrete, or other materials; and the shields block in all but a small fraction of the radiation which results from the reactor's operation. Nobody is allowed inside the reactor compartment while the reactor is turned on, and normally crewmen must wait twenty or thirty minutes after it is turned off before they reenter the area.* Radiation gauges tell them when the most intense radioactivity has died away.

Nuclear radiation is invisible; and you can't smell it, taste it, or weigh it. Nevertheless, it is easy to detect with modern instruments. Radiation monitors aboard U.S. Navy submarines are so sensitive that crew members are forbidden to wear wristwatches with radium-coated numerals. The small amount of radioactivity they give off would interfere with the measurements which are being made constantly. In fact, sailors aboard a nuclear sub are normally exposed to less radiation on a cruise than they get during shore duty. And the passengers who used to

---

* On some submarines, however, there is a thick, lead-glass window in the deck above the reactor; and crewmen can use it to see inside. Reactors may also be equipped with closed-circuit TV monitors.

Dials and gauges warn reactor operators of potential problems. This is the control room of Otto Hahn.

sun themselves around the edge of *Savannah*'s swimming pool regularly received more radiation (in the form of natural cosmic rays) than the reactor crew was getting in the control room below.

Considering the way nuclear fissions multiply in a chain reaction, one might wonder about the possibility of a "runaway reaction." Reactor designers have considered that prospect and have done things to prevent it. Start-up procedures are as formalized as the countdown for a space launch. The reactor crew won't begin any step on the list until all those that come before it have been taken and checked in the proper order. Dozens of the dials on the control console of the reactor are put there just so that the operators can tell at a glance if anything unusual is taking place. If it is, they customarily have several different methods of shutting the reactor down instantly—a procedure called a "scram."

Not everything is left to the crew's decisions, either. Most reactors will "scram" themselves automatically whenever instruments detect certain conditions. This will normally happen under the following circumstances:

120

(1) if the nuclear reaction rate increases suddenly, (2) if water temperature rises above a certain point, (3) if water pressure goes either too high or too low, (4) if a pipe breaks or the pumps stop, and (5) if the normal supply of electrical power to the control rods or to safety circuits fails, etc. In any of those cases, the control rods go zinging automatically back into the core—making it impossible for a chain reaction to continue. Nor are the control rods the only means of stopping the reactor. Another method is to dump in a neutron-absorbing material like boric acid. That would rarely be necessary, however. Most reactors are designed so that a chain reaction will end even if one or two of the control rods should get stuck on the way in. Reactors are "overdesigned" for safety.

So far as we know, no major reactor accident of any kind has ever taken place on a nuclear ship of any nation.* Even if it did, though, the gas-tight containment shell and the multiple layers of shielding would be expected to keep much radioactivity from escaping.

Radioactive materials that build up *inside* the reactor are a different problem. The most intense collection of them is sealed up inside the fuel elements themselves. Fission products like strontium-90 are formed in the ceramic fuel, but that is separated from the coolant by a sturdy, corrosion-resistant metal cladding. When a ship reactor is refueled, the old bundles are removed one by one. Each is carried to a reprocessing plant inside a massive, heavy shipping cask—built to survive any conceivable accident which might occur on the way without spilling its "hot" contents.

A certain small amount of radioactivity *does* find its

---

* The most dangerous situation may have been caused by the liquid metal leaks aboard *Seawolf*, which were mentioned on page 40.

way out of the power plant during normal operation. For instance, even the highly purified water which circulates through the reactor as its moderator and coolant may eventually build up some impurities. Most of them are microscopic specks of metal; they wear off the moving parts of pumps and other such equipment. Under the intense barrage of neutrons inside the core itself, however, these particles may become "activated." The water is constantly passing through demineralizing filters, and they trap most of this material. Still, new radioactivity is always appearing; so there is bound to be some in the reactor water at any given time. Besides, something must

The U.S. Navy's nuclear submarines are equipped with automatic washers and driers, but clothing worn in the reactor area is returned to port for separate laundering.

Crewmen on a nuclear sub practice the use of emergency breathing apparatus.

be done eventually with the radioactive stuff which builds up in the demineralizers. It is absorbed in a gummy material which must be replaced several times a year.

One thing that should be made clear is that the amount of radioactivity here is quite small. Admiral Rickover has testified before Congress that reactor cooling water on U.S. Navy ships normally runs—at full power—at or near the level which public health officials would consider okay for people to drink. Nevertheless, it is treated as "low level radioactive waste." The water in the reactor is sampled at least once a day, and its exact radioactivity is measured. At least once a week, an addi-

When a nuclear sub starts its reactor, heat causes the coolant water to expand. Excess may not be pumped into a harbor, however, without permission and a radiation check to make sure it's safe.

tional sample is taken which is allowed to "decay" for about five days before checking it with a Geiger-Müller counter. That gives short-lived radioactivity time to die away, so that only the longer-lived (and thus potentially more dangerous) radioactivity is recorded. If any of the tests show activity much above normal, the standing instruction is to look for the cause at once and to eliminate it if possible.

During ordinary operations, very little of the coolant water is removed from the reactor, so the volume of this "waste" isn't too great. There is one time when a fairly large volume of reactor water has to be removed; that's when the reactor is allowed to cool down completely and then is started up again. The water level in a reactor is usually kept constant, by adding "make-up water" as needed. When cool water is heated, however, it expands. During start-up of a submarine reactor, several hundred gallons of the coolant water may have to be drained off in a short time. Aboard a nuclear carrier, this could amount to thousands of gallons.

Because the radioactivity is so low, it's hard to imagine a situation in which this water couldn't be pumped into the open sea without risking any serious environmental damage (in case holding tanks were not available on board). The movement of the sea would dilute it quickly and thoroughly, so that it would really be "a drop in the ocean." It is likely to be just as safe when the ship is tied up at a dock, too; but there the rules must be stricter. Some radioactive elements tend to build up in fish and seaweed; some can cause more biological damage than others; some maintain their radioactivity for longer periods. All these factors are taken into account when standards are established by the International Commission on Radiological Protection; different limits are set for the permissible concentration of various materials. To simplify matters, the U.S. Navy has long assumed that *all* of the radioactivity in its coolant wastes is the nastiest kind—the long-lived, high-potency kind that tends to reconcentrate. Only if the radiation level falls into the "acceptable" range by those standards is a ship commander authorized to dispose of the excess coolant in the harbor. Otherwise, the overflow must be pumped into a tank on shore and hauled away to an approved disposal site—perhaps in another part of the country.

Over the years, the U.S. Public Health Service has checked the results at the handful of ports in this country where nuclear ships dock regularly. Neither the air nor the water in those areas has shown any increase over the radiation level which is natural in each locality. In some cases there was a slight increase of radioactivity in the mud on the bottom near the piers, but even that has dropped off in recent years. Surveys at nuclear sub bases in Spain and Scotland showed similar results. By introducing better equipment and by taking even greater care, Navy nukes now put a total of only about one percent as much radioactivity into harbor waters as they did in the early 1960's—even though far more nuclear ships are operating now.

Methods of handling the gunk from demineralizers on Navy ships have also changed. The original rule was that it had to be carried ashore if a ship was in port when the time came for a change. It was okay to dump the used filters into the ocean outside the 12-mile limit, however, if certain precautions were observed. Besides being at least about 20 kilometers from shore, the ship had to make sure that no other vessels were nearby and that the area was not a known fishing ground. The ship itself also had to be moving while the material was being released, to encourage quick mixing and dilution. Later, as the world's nuclear fleet grew, more conditions were added. The ship's commander also had to determine that the waters in the area were at least 200 fathoms deep (1,200 feet or more than 365 meters). This meant that the ship would be out beyond the edge of any "continental shelf."

In 1959, at the very beginning of the Atomic Shipping Age, the National Academy of Sciences in this country had suggested that it would be perfectly acceptable to get rid of demineralizer resins at sea. With more than one hundred propulsion reactors operating, the U.S. Navy found that it was still disposing of less radioactive material altogether in this way than the Academy had proposed as a reasonable limit *for each ship in a three-hundred-ship fleet*. Nevertheless, the Navy announced in 1970 that it would end ocean dumping of the gunk from its nukes completely. The resins are always brought back to port now. They are delivered to one of the officially supervised places on shore where they can be buried. This is what had always been done with other solid wastes—like old protective clothing, wiping rags, or equipment which somehow has become contaminated

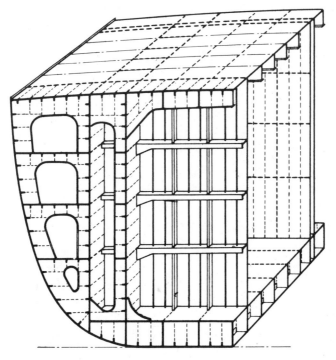

"Egg-crate type" construction strengthens the hulls of nuclear ships.

with radioactivity.* And this is what the commercial nukes like *Savannah* have always done with their demineralizing filters.

Normal reactor safety is only one of the goals of the nuclear ship program, however. There is also the problem of avoiding sea hazards. Somewhere in the world, a merchant ship is lost practically every day in a fire, colli-

---

* One exception was mentioned on page 40—equipment from the original *Seawolf* power plant. Another exception was allowed for many years in Hawaii, where the islands' volcanic rock makes land burial impractical. The AEC, the U.S. Public Health Service, and Hawaii's Department of Health approved a spot in the ocean more than 50 miles from shore, where the water was known to be approximately 15,000 feet deep. Low-level wastes were usually sealed in steel drums, which were then filled with concrete before being dropped at the site. The Navy used the place only ten times but stopped doing so in 1968. Now such wastes are brought to the U.S. mainland for disposal.

sion, wreck, sinking, or some other accident. Traveling on the ocean may not be as dangerous as driving on busy highways, but it is still risky.

Special rules apply to the way nuclear ships are built and operated. In 1960 the International Conference on the *Safety of Life at Sea* (sometimes called the "SOLAS" Conference) added a section to its recommendations which applies specifically to nukes. Lloyd's Register of Shipping—which helps to determine worldwide insurance rates on ships by the way it classifies them—devotes a separate chapter to nuclear shipping in its guidelines.

According to the SOLAS document (which was brought up to date in 1966), certain parts of a nuclear ship can't be riveted together; they must be *welded.* Heavier plating and thicker girders are to be used, too—even a specific type of "notch-tough" steel in the deck areas around the reactor itself. The SOLAS guide insists that a nuclear ship should be able to stay afloat and stable even if two of its main watertight compartments, right next to each other, are completely flooded. Nuclear ship designs feature double or triple hulls, as well as expensive "egg crate type" construction which gives extra protection.

In addition to all that, nuclear ships tend to be safer than conventional vessels because they almost invariably are supplied with the most modern equipment. It only makes sense to safeguard the heavy capital investment in a nuclear ship by giving it the best navigation facilities available, the latest collision-avoidance equipment, stabilizing devices, stress sensors, automated fire-detection and firefighting equipment.

Extra care in selecting the captain and crew of a nuclear ship is another factor. Just as passenger ships traditionally tend to have better safety records than others because the men who operate them recognize their greater responsibility, the same is true of nukes. Extra training is involved, too. U.S. Navy schools use realistic reproductions of shipboard equipment to train nuclear ships' crews on shore, and emergency situations are simulated from time to time to accustom the crew to react properly.

Aboard either a nuclear warship or a peaceful nuke, crewmen are drilled to check and test the ship's gear continually. This applies to conventional equipment as well as to the nuclear propulsion system. In this country, merchant ships are also subject to periodic safety inspections by the U.S. Coast Guard. At first, such reviews of N.S. *Savannah* took about a month, but later the annual inspection was streamlined to less than two weeks.

Ships of the U.S. Navy don't need operating licenses from any civilian agency, of course. It is also more difficult to find out about their safety procedures, because of military secrecy. Presumably, however, the Department of Defense is bound by the strict new laws about environmental protection in this country. The Nuclear Navy will have to be just as careful as everybody else in safeguarding the air and water, as well as in protecting public health and safety. Considering the strictness of the nuclear operating regulations which the Navy *has* revealed, this shouldn't be a great problem.

Regardless of all these precautions, problems do appear and ship accidents do occur—even to nukes. Fires and explosions have taken place aboard them, including a major disaster on the biggest one of all in January, 1969. An air-to-ground rocket aboard *Enterprise* overheated and blew up, while the carrier was at sea about 75 miles from Honolulu. Other blasts followed as nine bombs exploded, ripping holes in the flight deck; and fires broke out. Twenty-eight crewmen died, and the big ship was

A series of explosions and fires damaged Enterprise *during maneuvers in 1969, but the nuclear power plant was not involved.*

out of action for nearly two months.* Yet there was never any threat that radioactivity would be released.

Collisions take place, too. The submarine *Seadragon* hit a whale during her first sea trials. In 1962 another sub (*Permit*) was cruising just beneath the surface off the California coast when it rammed a freighter. In fact, two nuclear submarines have even bumped into each other. That happened to *Barb* and *Sargo* in October, 1965. *Sargo* has had more than its share of misfortune; a few years earlier it was damaged by a flash fire while loading liquid oxygen at Pearl Harbor. There have been other incidents like these, and they have occurred on foreign ships as well as those of the United States. The important

---

* The bombs carried as much explosive as half a dozen submarine cruise missiles. If *Enterprise* had suffered damage like this during a battle cruise, Navy officers say that the deck would have been cleared and—after a few hours of temporary repairs—the carrier could have resumed fighting.

thing is that they have never caused any extra damage or danger because they happened to take place on nuclear-propelled ships.

Both Russian and U.S. nuclear subs have been lost at sea, although the two cases which attracted the most attention were the ones which involved American ships—the 1963 sinking of *Thresher* and the loss of *Scorpion* in 1968. Nobody aboard survived either tragedy; but, so far as later investigations could determine, neither sinking was caused by any failure in the nuclear propulsion systems. Once the wreckage of each sub was located, seawater in the area and mud from the ocean bottom nearby was tested for radioactivity. The readings were normal, indicating that fission products from inside the reactors hadn't caused contamination in either case.

The position of the reactor on a nuclear ship is one of its safeguards. The reactor is normally near the middle of the ship, where stresses are lowest and where the reactor compartment is most likely to stay intact even if the ship breaks up. It is usually surrounded by collision barriers of some sort, and *Otto Hahn* added another protective feature. The reactor area aboard the German ship is ringed by a series of extra-strength "cutting decks." The idea behind this design is that if another ship rammed the nuclear vessel at high speed the bow of the first ship would be sliced into pieces or at least blunted before it got near the reactor containment. That would cushion the impact and keep the intruding bow from punching through the innermost walls around the reactor.

A reactor's vapor-tight pressure vessel is another safety factor, even if the nuclear ship should sink. *Thresher* went down in more than 8,000 feet of water; it was still deeper in the place southwest of the Azores where *Scorpion* met her end. Many containers might be crushed by the weight of the water at such depths, but a reactor ves-

Thresher *(above)* *was the first nuclear ship reported lost. The in-vestigation after its sinking led to tighter supervision over manu-facturing techniques and a few changes in ship procedures, but an examination of its wreckage on the sea bottom (below) showed its loss had nothing to do with its nuclear reactor.*

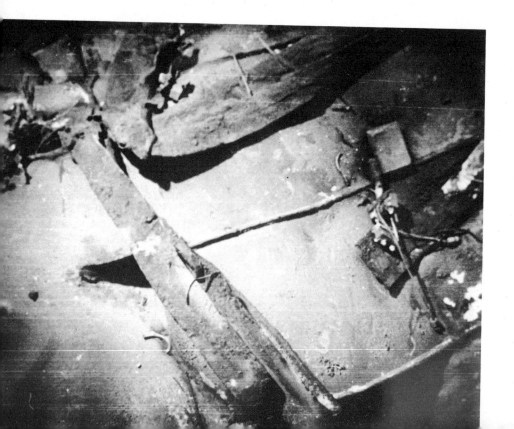

sel is probably heavy enough to withstand it. Even if the reactor container should fail, the cladding of the fuel elements themselves offers yet another means of sealing in the radioactive fission products. This is one reason why the fuel cladding is always an alloy which corrodes very, very slowly—even in seawater.

Considering all these facts, it seems strange that people go on protesting so much about nuclear ship safety. Some Japanese still object to visits by U.S. Navy nukes, and *Savannah* never was permitted to dock in that country. The New York City Council recently considered a complete ban on nuclear ships. *Otto Hahn* was long restricted to German ports, because other countries were slow in granting it permission to enter their harbors. Part of the problem is misinformation, but there is also a lack of worldwide agreement on what to do in case there ever *is* a serious nuclear accident involving a ship.

Some of the attitudes in Japan are purely emotional. They are mixed up with the terrible memories of Hiroshima and Nagasaki, and also with opposition to the Vietnamese war and to U.S. military involvement in Asia. In

A Russian "N Class" submarine surfaces in distress. It is believed that the sub eventually sank, although the crew was rescued.

the case of an incident at Sasebo in 1968, there also appears to have been a simple error in measurement. The event is worth describing because it illustrates how difficult it may be to change people's minds about nuclear energy.

Japanese government technicians were in a small boat in Sasebo Harbor monitoring radiation in the water about 100 yards from the nuclear submarine *Swordfish*. Suddenly the readings jumped. The measurements were still far below the limits which the International Commission on Radiological Protection recommends as acceptable for public exposures, and within minutes the readings went back to normal. The higher readings were never repeated. Nevertheless, the incident was widely publicized; and Japanese officials insisted that *Swordfish* must have done something improper. The Prime Minister demanded an immediate investigation. High-ranking representatives of the U.S. Atomic Energy Commission and the Navy flew to the scene, and a study of the situation showed that the readings had probably been faulty—caused either by radar or by electronic interference from welding operations on a repair ship between the small boat and the sub. The reactor on *Swordfish* had been shut down for several days before the incident, and nothing in the water or bottom sediments around the ship indicated that any radioactive material had been released—either intentionally or accidentally. Nevertheless, diplomats trembled. U.S. nuclear ships were barred from bases in Japan for more than seven months, while Japanese authorities ordered and installed new air-monitoring equipment. Eventually the Japanese agreed that electronic interference *could* produce inaccurate readings momentarily.* So they gave the Navy a

---

* The same sort of interference might occur on a nuclear ship itself, but it would be too small to bother the most important measuring systems and it would probably be recognized by an experienced operator in other cases.

list of equipment which U.S. crews were not to use while nuclear ships were in port; it included radar, radiography, and X-ray systems. The Navy resisted, but the Japanese were equally stubborn. The matter dragged on for years, and maybe we haven't yet heard the last of it. All this trouble arose over a mistaken reading—of a radiation level which wouldn't have indicated danger if it *had* existed.

The Japanese attitude toward nuclear ships will probably change as *Mutsu* begins regular operation. Certainly it will have to become more realistic when the German-Japanese nukes go into service.

The problem of getting clearance for peaceful nukes to enter other countries' ports still is a complicated one. The International Atomic Energy Agency (a special body of the United Nations) has suggested for years that a single set of guidelines be adopted universally but so far permission still must be negotiated country by country. The European Nuclear Energy Agency also is working on a model agreement for visiting arrangements. When general rules are eventually adopted, they will probably be relatively simple:

(1) Nuclear ships will have to certify that they meet certain internationally established standards in design, construction, and crew training.

(2) A safety assessment will have to be prepared for each port a ship will visit, and this will have to be submitted to local officials in advance. There are enough differences in currents, tides, meteorological conditions, harbor traffic, etc., so that each docking area would be considered a different "operating site" for a nuclear reactor.

(3) It will be forbidden for a ship to discharge radioactive liquids, gases, or solids in the port area unless this is specifically authorized by the harbor authorities before the action takes place.

(4) Each ship will carry documents showing that periodic

inspections have been made on all its important equipment and that they are all in good order—including the emergency, nonnuclear propulsion system which can move the ship without using its reactor.

(5) Some agreement will have to be reached about liability in case of accidents.

This final point is a tough one, partly because there has never been a nuclear accident. Ship insurance seems high anyway; a 250,000-ton oil tanker pays more than a million dollars a year in premiums. But at least that payment can be based on actual experience. Lloyd's of London and other companies know how much damage might be expected from a waterfront fire or an oil spill. It's harder to estimate what the effect of a fantastically improbable nuclear ship accident might be, in which large amounts of radioactivity escaped and had to be cleaned up.

It seems to be accepted generally that in a case like this

Longshoremen who loaded and unloaded Savannah *were paid at regular rates because it was decided that no special hazard was associated with the nuclear ship.*

the owners or operators of a nuclear ship would be required to pay for *all* damages. It wouldn't matter whether the nuclear ship had been at fault, whether the blame belonged to somebody else, or whether the whole affair was just an act of God. Yet there must be *some* limit to this sort of liability. And as soon as a dollar limit is set—no matter how high—someone complains that it isn't high enough. In the case of *Otto Hahn*, one of Germany's small neighbors raised a further question: Suppose the same accident should cause damage in Belgium and the Netherlands at the same time. If Germany had agreed with each country to accept liability up to a certain amount, would the total liability be doubled because two countries were involved? (Probably not.)

The U.S. Congress passed special legislation for N.S. *Savannah*. It gave that ship the same government promise to meet damage claims which is provided for land-based nuclear power plants. Combined with commercial insurance, the coverage goes up to $560,000,000. The government pledge isn't completely free; companies that get it pay a fee. But this isn't exactly an insurance premium either. It isn't based on statistical tables, because there have been no accidents; and the chances of having one are considered so slight that the government really doesn't expect to lose anything. Nevertheless, legitimate claims *would* be paid if they were made, and the federal guarantee is unquestioned.

The subject of financial liability is often brought up by critics of nuclear propulsion. Just because it is complex and involves such staggeringly large sums of money, they suggest that this means nuclear ships are unsafe. Actually, it doesn't mean that at all. There is one simple, straightforward, and accurate answer to the old question: "How safe are nuclear ships?"

They are *safe enough*!

CHAPTER SEVEN

20,000,000 Leagues Under Nuclear Power

W hat is life like for the crew of a nuclear ship? What special training does a nuclear sailor need? What are his duties?

The answers vary from ship to ship, of course, but not as much as you might expect. Naturally, there are differences between a military ship and a civilian one, or between a surface vessel and a sub. But a fairly good overall picture can be based on a close look at just one category —the ballistic-missile-firing submarines. Service aboard them is more demanding than on any other type of nuke. Furthermore, the FBM submarines of the world's four nuclear navies are similar to one another in many ways, and they make up nearly half of the world's atomic fleet.

In the U.S., British, and French navies, each of these big subs has two complete crews. The crews take turns operating the ship so that the mobile ICBM bases can stay on underwater patrol most of the time. Although the Russians won't say so officially, they almost surely follow a similar pattern. The strain of operating in total isolation on such a continuously important mission might reduce a crew's efficiency if the men did not have a break at least every two or three months.

Submariners aboard U.S. missile subs alternate every

U.S. ballistic missile sub Sam Houston *returns to Holy Loch, Scotland, to switch crews after a patrol in the Mediterranean.*

sixty days; and the crew switch often takes place at an overseas port (such as Holy Loch, Scotland, or Rota, Spain). In that way, the submarine loses less time from its assigned area.

The two distinct crews are equal in every way. For this reason they aren't called the first and second crew, or Crew A and Crew B. They are designated by the Navy's official colors—a "Blue Crew" and a "Gold Crew."

While one crew is on patrol, the other stays busy in the United States. Some officers and enlisted men may take leave, but most attend refresher courses which keep them up to date on ever-changing technical subjects. It's important for a sub's crew to work together smoothly, so there is also some team-training with those men who will join the ship for the first time on the next cruise or who will be handling new assignments. Because of promotions and transfers, about one sailor in six on a U.S. sub patrol is new to the ship.

A few days before the crew switch, the entire group of perhaps one hundred and thirty-five men is flown to the port where the changeover will take place. The two crews meet briefly so that the new group can learn of any problems which might have arisen during the patrol. Then, after several weeks of normal maintenance work and a short trial run to make sure everything is working properly, the big sub steams out to sea again. Once it dives beneath the surface to begin its patrol, nobody should see it or hear from it again for sixty days.

(So far, no nuclear *surface* ship has used a double crew, but the system has been suggested for the U.S. Navy's atomic aircraft carriers. Its purpose would be the same as with missile subs—to make it easier for a ship to stay on duty continuously for a long time. The entire crew of a huge vessel like *Enterprise* or *Nimitz* wouldn't have to be replaced at once; it might make more sense to switch men back and forth in smaller working groups. Eventually, some sort of relief-crew system might even be worked out for commercial nukes. Too much money is invested in building nuclear ships to allow them to stand idle unnecessarily.)

At the time a U.S. ballistic missile sub leaves port, its crew can assume that the voyage will take a couple of months—during which the sub and its missiles must be ready for action instantly at any time of the day or night. Depending on the type of duty, a crewman's work shift may last anywhere from four to twelve hours.

"Day" and "night" would lose meaning on submarine patrols if it weren't for the lights. During hours which correspond to normal darkness above, the white fluores-

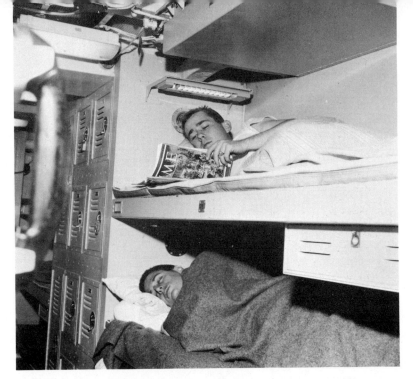

Each man aboard George Washington *has a private locker next to his bunk, which is roomy by submarine standards.*

cent tubes in many parts of the ship are turned off. The dimmer red glow of the lights which replace them gives a nighttime feeling; and this traditional cycle of light and dark makes the strange surroundings seem more natural. It also keeps eyes adapted to night use of the periscope.

This game with lights doesn't affect the sub's basic assignment to stay alert around the clock. At any given moment, between 30 percent and 50 percent of the crew is on duty. But, whether they are working or relaxing, the nuclear submariners spend their patrol time in an atmosphere which is as pleasant as it can be made.

The most obvious difference between a nuclear sub and a diesel is the former's roominess. There are batteries aboard for emergency use—up to 100 tons of them; but space which would be occupied on a diesel sub by fuel oil can be devoted on a nuke to making the undersea ship more livable as well as more effective. Only the captain

141

has a room all to himself, but the bunk beds for crew members are a huge improvement over the narrow ledges and hammocks of the old days. Except on rare missions (when extra crewmen, trainees or passengers must be carried for some reason), the practice of "hot bunking" has disappeared. Subs used to be so cramped that two men sometimes had to alternate in a single sleeping space. Now privacy has reached the point that every berth has an individual reading lamp and ventilation control. Each area has its own switches for the "piped" music on board.

The officers' lounge (which the U.S. Navy calls a "ward room") is nearly as big as the eating and recreation space once was for an entire sub crew. There are even real stairways in some parts of the nuke rather than the traditional skinny ladders.

Enough movies are carried on board so that a different one can be shown each day—often on a Cinemascope screen. There is a substantial library . . . and perhaps a piano. Pastel colors everywhere—pale blue, pale green,

Garlic bread, salad, spaghetti, and meatballs make an afternoon meal aboard John Adams.

gray and tan—make compartments aboard the ship look even bigger. Wood-grained formica paneling adds to the hominess, and oil paintings or framed prints sometimes add distinctive decoration.

Good food helps to keep men's spirits up. The chow aboard the fleet subs is considered the best in the Navy. There may be no T-bone steaks (boneless meat is preferred, to cut down on storage volume); but the meals are appetizing, varied, colorful, and hearty. Four meals are served regularly each day, with the extra one coming near midnight, just before the late night movie on some ships. This means that enough supplies must be carried to prepare up to 32,400 meals during a normal patrol (135 men $\times$ 4 meals $\times$ 60 days). Plus a bit more. The galleys are always open in case anybody wants to fix himself a quick snack. And there's an ice cream machine on board, too.

To help keep its submariners from swelling up like balloons, the Navy provides opportunities for exercise. There is no basketball court (as there may be aboard a giant surface nuke); but at least there is gymnasium equipment. Because a missile sub is considerably more than a city block long, crewmen also have a chance to move around quite a bit. This provides exercise and helps to prevent monotony. Walks around the ship can be a form of training, too. It isn't unusual to see a sailor or an officer "walking the pipes" with a diagram in his hand to learn more about details of the ship. It takes time and perseverance; there are nearly 50 miles of piping inside an FBM submarine.

Submarine sailors are generally a healthy group. After the first few days of patrol, even colds disappear. Everybody on board builds up a natural resistance to the limited number of germs present, and there is no danger of fresh infection. This means, however, that the men may

An exercise bike helps keep nuclear sailors trim.

pick up the sniffles easily when they reenter the less sanitary "real world" at the end of a patrol. In case of more serious illnesses emergency surgery can take place without interrupting a mission, and many an operation has been performed beneath the surface of the ocean. Thanks to modern medicines and regular checkups, however, this happens much more rarely than in the early days, when each missile sub was required to carry a doctor.

The seas in which a sub "lives" are important for its

survival. As it moves through the depths, the ship gulps in hundreds of gallons each minute. Much of it is needed to cool its condensers, its generators, and its air-conditioning apparatus, but some of it also becomes the ship's main source of air and fresh water.

Seawater is broken up into hydrogen and oxygen by electrolysis to replenish the breathing supply. Some water goes to a distillation unit, which removes the salt and produces fresh water for drinking, cooking, and bathing. Unlike either the subs or surface ships of old, the nukes don't need to ration showers.

Humidity and temperature aboard a nuclear sub are kept at comfortable levels. The air is clean. Odors are removed before air is recirculated, and there is practically no dust.

Air-conditioning on a modern sub is complicated but effective. Unlike a spaceship or a diver's helmet, which may use *pure* oxygen, the sub keeps an atmosphere of ordinary air—a mixture of oxygen and nitrogen. Inside the thick hull, the air pressure is the same as it would be in port, so there is no danger of getting the "bends" from diving and surfacing quickly. The air is recirculated constantly, however, so the carbon dioxide exhaled by the men on board must be removed on a continuous basis. This is done by "scrubbers," in which chemicals absorb the carbon dioxide and some other impurities while letting the oxygen pass through. The carbon dioxide which has been removed is replaced by additional oxygen, and both the humidity and the temperature of the fresh mixture are kept at a comfortable level. This may be as important to the sensitive electronic gear aboard as it is to the men.

Like astronauts, the submariners must follow certain rules to keep from contaminating their self-contained atmosphere. For example, aerosol cans may not be used

H.M.S. Repulse *at Plymouth, England. Notice the underwater stabilizers at various points on the hull.*

for shaving cream, deodorant, dessert topping, or anything else on board. The freon gas in such cans is heavier than air and would tend to collect in the lowest parts of the sub, where it would make breathing difficult and uncomfortable. Ordinary mercury thermometers are forbidden, too—for fear that they might break and release a poisonous vapor into the air-conditioning system. To help keep the air clean, sub crewmen wear lintless dacron coveralls while on patrol. In fact, they are even urged to wear lint-free underwear. Laundry is no great problem aboard today's submarines, by the way, because there are automatic washers and dryers. The luxury of ample power from a nuclear reactor extends to little things as well as big ones.

Electrolyzing water seems like the most obvious way for a nuclear submarine to get its oxygen, but this system was not used on the earliest nukes. They carried liquefied oxygen in metal tanks and also replenished their air sup-

146

ply occasionally through snorkel tubes like those mentioned on page 44. For brief emergencies, they counted on a special kind of candle, which *gives off* oxygen as it burns instead of using it up. It soon became clear that nukes didn't need such relics of the past, however; and now the subs are so completely independent that long underwater cruises can be considered routine.

The ride aboard a nuclear sub is a smooth one for the most part. Staying well below the surface waters, the ship can forget about winds and waves. Yet there can still be sudden jolts. When a crewman hears the rough shriek of the diving signal—*A-oooo-gah!* *A-ooo-gah!*—he braces himself instinctively. Subs can also bank or turn suddenly; and more than once an unexpected maneuver has left spaghetti and meatballs dripping from the walls and ceiling (or, as the Navy insists on calling them, the "bulkheads" and "overhead").

After all, the nuclear submariners are not aboard just for the ride. Nearly one-third of them are assigned specifically to jobs involving the ballistic missiles carried by the sub. About the same number take care of the nuclear power plant. The rest have an assortment of duties, ranging from maintenance of electronic equipment to manning the torpedo tubes in case of a sea battle.

Although no nuclear submarine has ever launched its missiles at a real enemy, every patrol involves drills. Without warning, the crew must prepare in minutes for firing. More than 95 percent of the time, the U.S. Navy reports that such checkups show all sixteen missiles aboard each of its subs are ready to go. Not even one time in one hundred does a serious problem develop with more than one missile aboard any given ship. An "electronic watchman" scans the missiles and fire-control equipment continuously during each voyage, reporting any piece which isn't functioning properly. Usually, re-

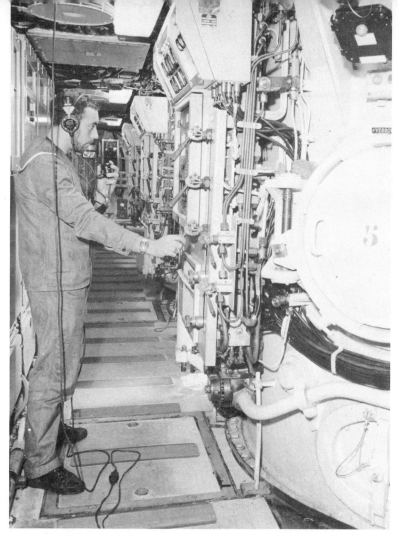

pairs can be made simply by inserting a new plug-in tray of circuits and transistors. The automated "watchman" even watches itself; it can check over its own components to make sure that the inspection is being carried out correctly.

The long-range rockets themselves stand in vertical tubes, rising like rows of massive tree trunks from a midship area nicknamed "Sherwood Forest." Repairs and adjustments can be made through small doors in each tube; there is a door on each of the three decks which surround the missiles. The launch controls are in another section of the sub, farther forward.

Missile areas aboard French, United States, and British subs show many similarities. (Above), U.S.S. Lafayette; (below), H.M.S. Resolution; (opposite), the French Foudroyant.

A sub should be able to fire its missiles at the rate of about one a minute, and they may be destined for many different targets. To do its job, the sub must know its own position perfectly. It keeps track of its position primarily by means of an inertial navigation system, like the kind developed originally for aerospace programs. Using several gyroscopes, this Ship Inertial Navigation System (SINS) measures the vessel's acceleration in any direction (including upward or downward). A computer puts all the information together instantly, so the exact distance and direction from the sub's known starting point is al-

A U.S. sub with missile hatches open. An inner cover keeps rocket dry on a submerged sub until firing, then shatters as the missile is popped upward by compressed gas.

ways known. The fire-control apparatus, which recalculates the planned missile trajectories every few seconds, is so sensitive that it takes into account the effects of the earth's rotation. Yet accuracy is too important to risk *any* mistake. No single inertial navigation system is trusted completely by a missile sub. There are two or three such systems aboard, so that one can be matched against another. In addition, a sub may break the surface occasionally with its "star tracking periscope." This device requires only a quick glimpse of the sky to double-check the ship's current location. If the sky is overcast, a midget version of a radio telescope is used to spot the radiation of otherwise invisible stars—so celestial navigation is still possible. Finally, each sub has radio receivers which record the signals from beacon stations on shore or from satellites as they pass within range. Both the United States and the USSR have navigation satellites, and the orbits of each are calculated so painstakingly that they serve as "nearby stars"—making it possible to determine a ship's position within a few yards.

Obviously the sub needs its own computers with which to operate all these systems. In fact, there are *dozens* of computers aboard. The nuke needs a well-trained crew, too. Crewmen on U.S. missile subs are almost invariably at least high school graduates. Their average age (including all officers) is less than twenty-five; and many take advantage of filmed lectures to earn extra college credits while serving on patrol.

The Navy likes to boast that there is room on a nuclear submarine for everything but mistakes. That's not far from the truth. Life aboard is pleasant, but the potential perils never vanish completely while traveling hundreds of feet below the surface. And any error with the missiles could be especially tragic. This is why the extremely rare report of drug use by submariners is alarming. Even aside from that, there is always the danger that a crewman could go berserk, or try to commit sabotage, or just goof. Because of all these possibilities, every major system on the sub has some sort of backup. And to prevent the accidental launch of a missile, it takes at least two men (including the commanding officer) to arm any warhead and carry out the firing process. The access doors used to repair or replace missile parts are normally kept locked, and a warning light flashes on a master control board whenever one is opened.

Once a missile sub begins its patrol, it is more remote in some ways than a rocket ship in space. It can *receive* radio messages (even when submerged, by using the right frequencies and a relatively slow code); but it is

A French submariner plots his ship's course, based on data from a number of navigation systems.

Submarines on patrol try to keep track of other ships in the area through passive sonar without being spotted themselves.

forbidden to use its transmitter. Breaking radio silence would give away its own position. A possible enemy could zero in on the outgoing signal. There are half a dozen different sonar systems aboard the sub—including the kind that send out a pinging noise and identify objects from the echoes which bounce back—but even that sound is forbidden while actually on patrol. Only "passive" sonar is permitted then. The operators merely sit and listen. They soon become accustomed to the clicking of shrimp, to the grunts and groans of whales, to the shrieks and squeaks and chirps and whistles of different varieties of fish. But they can also hear the sounds of other ships, while doing their best to stay unheard and unnoticed themselves.

Military subs must even be sure to hide their garbage. All waste material from the ship is crammed into weighted bags of fine plastic mesh, which won't rise to the surface after being blown out through a tube by compressed air. A trail of trash behind a sub would be too easy for planes or surface ships to spot.

By letting an antenna float above it, a U.S. sub can pick up news broadcasts by Armed Forces Radio. It also receives brief personal messages from home for crew members. These "Familygrams" are continuously mixed with military messages and sent in similar code. In that way, other ships listening to the radio signals beamed toward an area patrolled by nuclear subs can get no hint of an increase or decrease in incoming military orders. But the sub itself never responds. If a missile sub ran into trouble during the early part of a patrol, it might sink without being missed for weeks.

In spite of these grim features, the spirit aboard a nuclear sub is likely to be high. The ships' newspapers are often spiced with humor. If a U.S. crew gets a chance to surface near the North Pole, you can bet that someone

Gigantic antenna systems like this one—covering 2,800 acres at Cutler, Maine—can broadcast messages to submerged subs. This transmitter uses very low radio frequencies and is forty times as powerful as the largest commercial radio station in the U.S.

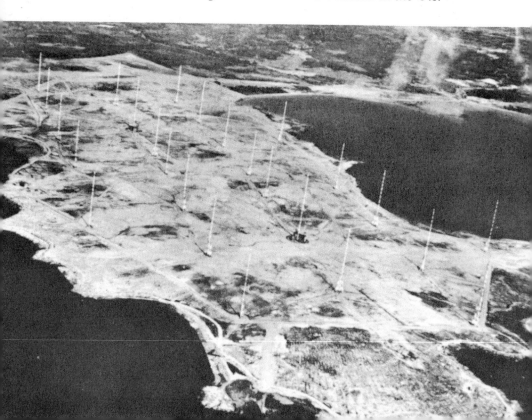

will whip up a quick baseball game on the ice pack. The Russians, in similar fashion, report that they have used such opportunities to hold ice-skating and ski competitions. Morale is not usually a big problem with any elite group, and nuclear seamen of all nations are picked with enough care to be considered an elite.

Operating the nuclear power plant itself is another full-time job. Whether the sub is moving ahead at full speed or just hovering, it depends on its reactor as a constant source of energy. At best, the power plant crew does little but watch dials and follow the routine of inspections, maintenance and drills. At worst, it may be plagued with leaky seals, temperamental pumps, faulty circuits, and jammed mechanical equipment. If the reactor has to be shut down for repairs, specialists may even enter the spotless white reactor compartment itself. Normally, however, the only view a nuclear sailor gets of the reactor is through a heavy, yellow, lead-glass window in the deck above it. For the most part, nuclear power is an unseen (but vital) presence.

Naturally, there are times when a nuclear sub needs more extensive care than it can get from its own crew while under way. Each country has its own types of support ships to help with these larger jobs. The United States uses floating dry docks in some foreign ports. It also has tenders which are equipped with heavy cranes to load missiles and "clean rooms" in which delicate electronic adjustments can be made. The Soviet Union's submarine support vessels are much smaller, but they are versatile and they stay on the move. They may remain on duty for half a year at a time in the patrol area itself, serving as seagoing repair shops. Each can take care of three or four subs at once. Continuous operation tends to wear nuclear subs out, however; and after about four years of service every nuke must return to a shipyard for

Nuclear submarine support vessels: (Above), the floating drydock
Los Alamos and (below) the U.S.S. Hunley. (Opposite), a Russian
"Echo" submarine on patrol near the Equator ties up alongside a
tender. The tanker beyond is servicing the tender.

a complete overhaul, which may take twelve months or more.

An account of life aboard a ballistic missile sub offers lots of clues to crew conditions aboard other nukes. Service on any of them is likely to be more plush than on a conventional ship of the same general type, but it is also more demanding. Intelligence and calm resourcefulness are probably more important than physical strength and stamina. More training is required to serve on a nuke than on a traditional steamship or motor vessel, and the servicing procedures in port or at sea are obviously quite different. All of this is true for either subs or surface ships —for military ships and the peaceful nukes as well.

Plumbers, machinists, and engine-maintenance men

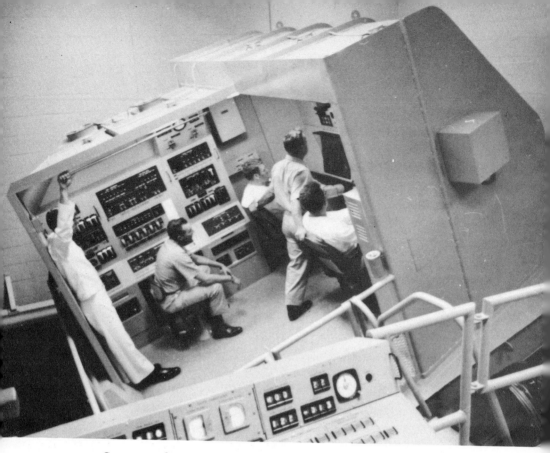

Crew members of a sub practice as a team on a land-based simulator.

must learn to work with alloys which aren't normally found to any large extent on conventional ships. Radiation monitoring and decontamination techniques are extra skills which must be acquired.

Land schools use realistic simulators to give trainees the feel of shipboard equipment (even including sound effects and vibration), but practice problems on shore are not quite the same as experience under way. That's when crewmen really have to be ready for the unexpected. And that's why Admiral Rickover developed a challenging test for the men on each new sub as it undergoes sea trials. Without warning, one person is ordered to "vanish" and someone else is required to take over his job

Local officials tour Enterprise *during the nuke's visit to Sierra Leone.*

immediately. It keeps people on their toes—which is where they should be.

Finally, public relations is a responsibility which can't be overlooked—even on military vessels. When visitors are permitted, or when legitimate questions are asked, the crew of any nuclear ship must be prepared to handle them. Even after hundreds of nukes have been built—even after they have traveled a total of nearly 20,000,000 leagues under nuclear power—they are still a curiosity.

CHAPTER EIGHT

Can Atomic Ships Make a Profit?

Deciding when to switch from fuel oil to nuclear reactors is a complicated matter. Yet the process is a lot like selecting a new automobile, and that's a type of decision-making most people understand. It's an interesting comparison to keep in mind when arguments for and against nuclear ships seem hard to unravel.

What is the key to picking a car? Gasoline mileage? Passenger space? Appearance? Quick pickup? Rugged construction? All are important, in varying degrees. A buyer probably won't find *everything* he wants in *any* single auto, so the final choice is difficult. Would it be better to have lots of head and leg room, or is it more important to have a car which fits into a small parking space? Above all, which of the many cars on the market can he afford? If he can spend only a limited amount of money, he may have to match a cheap model of one of the deluxe cars against the best produced by another manufacturer. Whether he realizes it or not, he may wind up trading some extra horsepower and a sporty silhouette for additional trunk space and long-term economy, or vice versa. Shipowners—military or nonmilitary—go through a similar process before deciding whether or not to order the "nuclear propulsion option." They ask themselves

Crewmen aboard Enterprise *spell out a famous equation. The Navy's formula for comparing the military effectiveness of nuclear and nonnuclear ships is a lot more complicated.*

what they really need, what either a nuke or a conventional ship offers, and what they can afford.

U.S. Department of Defense officials have formalized the system for comparing a nuclear ship with a conventional vessel. They ask a list of questions about each one, awarding a specific number of points for a "perfect" answer in each case and a lower score for responses which are less satisfactory. Totaling the score is like grading an examination; and the result is called the ship's "effectiveness factor." For an aircraft carrier, there are about a dozen basic questions, including these: How long will it take to respond to an emergency? How many plane flights can it launch within a ten-day period? How long can it

161

stick to its station in a battle zone? How vulnerable is it to attack by an enemy?

Clearly, a nuclear aircraft carrier is more effective than one of the same size using oil-fired boilers. The "effectiveness factor" assigned to *Enterprise* is 1.17, compared to 1.08 for a conventional carrier of similar size. But critics may argue that the questions should be scored differently. Who can say that a ship's speed in getting to a trouble spot is more or less important than its various operations after it arrives? To some extent, the ratings are still a matter of personal opinion.

Comparing costs is not simple. The price tag on a single nuclear aircraft carrier has risen to more than a billion dollars, but the precise amount depends on which items you count. When those who favor nuclear propulsion argue with those who oppose it, each side likes to use only the statistics which support its own view. For instance, an atomic-propelled carrier has room to carry more airplanes than a "comparable" conventional ship. Should the cost of buying extra planes be added to the nuke's basic construction expense? It's a tricky question —especially because the air armada aboard a carrier will eventually cost more than the vessel itself. (See figure opposite.)

Take another example. During its service life, a conventional carrier spends far more on fuel than does a nuke, but fuel oil is purchased gradually, over a period of years. Therefore, isn't the higher cost of the conventional fuel actually easier to manage? Maybe so.

Even the cost of fuel oil is hard to pin down, however. Warships often must take on fuel at sea, and delivery ships cost more to operate than their fuel load itself is worth at normal prices. A $2.50 barrel of oil costs the Navy more than $6 by the time it gets to a carrier.

Although nobody now questions the military effective-

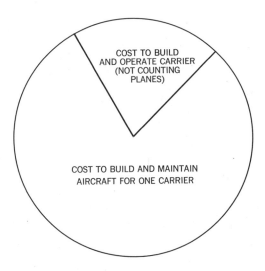

COST TO BUILD
AND OPERATE CARRIER
(NOT COUNTING
PLANES)

COST TO BUILD AND MAINTAIN
AIRCRAFT FOR ONE CARRIER

The extra expense of powering an aircraft carrier by nuclear energy instead of fossil fuel is only a small part of what it costs to build and operate a carrier for its normal thirty-year life. Planes are extremely expensive and are usually replaced every seven years.

ness and importance of nuclear submarines, their growing cost causes disputes, too. Taking into account the missiles on board, each one of the most advanced submarines now being planned by the United States will probably cost even more than a nuclear carrier. The enormous new subs will undoubtedly be built anyway, however, unless some worldwide agreement on disarmament is reached. The need for "effectiveness" is the most powerful single argument when any major nation plans its military budget.

Businessmen, on the other hand, look at nukes differently. The comparisons they must make are almost as intricate, but *all* of them relate to cost. You might say that the decision of whether or not to acquire a commercial nuke is less like buying a passenger car and more like buying a truck for business purposes.

The sort of truck you want depends on the sort of business you are in. You may need a huge van if you are hauling large equipment from one part of the country to another, but the same kind of vehicle would make no sense at all for delivering groceries from a neighborhood store. In the same way, nuclear propulsion is now a logical economic choice—but *only* for large ships which travel fairly long distances and which need a considerable amount of power. It would be wasteful to put a nuclear reactor into a small vessel which doesn't move around much. To understand why, it may help to continue this analogy between ships and trucks.

How much would it be worth to a truck owner if his trucks could be driven for two or three years at a time before stopping for gas? That would depend almost entirely on how much the magic fuel for these remarkable trucks cost him in the long run. The owner might welcome the convenience of eliminating fuel stops, but no truck fleet could afford to pay 35 percent extra in its purchase prices for this advantage alone. That percentage is roughly the difference between building several large nuclear merchant ships (*e.g.,* 250,000 deadweight-ton tankers) and building the same number of conventional ships of the same capacity.

Now suppose that the magic truck fuel we had imagined cost a lot less than the ordinary gasoline it replaced. It *still* isn't certain that the truck fleet owner would be interested. The economic reasons are simple:

First, his *total* costs might be the same or lower, but much of his money would always be tied up in fuel. It would be like saving ten cents a gallon on gasoline, but then paying a $300 deposit on the fuel tank in which he had to carry it. That is exactly the situation which may face a nuclear ship owner. The tiny amount of fuel the nuke "burns" must be kept in an expensive (though "returnable") container.

164

A fairly large amount of fissionable fuel material must always be present in the core of a nuclear reactor for it to operate. Otherwise, an energy-releasing chain reaction simply won't take place. Thus, a ship's reactor must be loaded with much more fuel than it can use up. To compare it with a truck again—in a slightly more precise way—it is as if the truck's engine would work only when the gas tank was at least half full.

As a reactor generates power, it also builds up "fission products" within its fuel. These are the nuclear fragments which result when fuel atoms are split apart. Fission products might be likened to sludge in a truck engine because they hamper the reactor's operation. By absorbing (and wasting) neutrons, the fission products make a reactor less and less efficient as it continues to operate. The reactor can put out heat just as well, but it wastes fuel doing so.

This economic penalty is ignored by military ships, which use very highly enriched fuel and simply load more fissionable material to begin with. To keep it from reacting too vigorously at first, the richer core also includes "burnable poisons"—which soak up the extra neutrons at the beginning but gradually disappear while fission products increase. By refueling only after ten years or so, warships sacrifice fuel efficiency in order to spend more time on active patrol duty.

Commercial ships can't afford to operate that way, even though the shipowner might be happier if his vessels *never* had to interrupt their work to switch reactor cores at all. Unfortunately, it costs money at each step—to load nuclear fuel, to use the fuel, to unload it again, and to have it reprocessed. Still, all things considered, the cheapest system is to refuel every two or three years; and that's what a smart ship operator will do. Furthermore, he will buy a richer nuclear fuel (like premium gasoline

165

for a truck) only if the reactor manufacturer and fuel supplier can demonstrate that this approach will be more profitable for him in the long run.

All this doesn't mean that the commercial nuke tries to burn its atomic fuel as efficiently as possible, however. Strangely enough, that might also cost the owner money. Fuel efficiency is usually measured in "megawatt-days per ton." This expression corresponds roughly to "miles per gallon" in a truck or car (or—if you want to be more precise—to "horsepower hours per gallon"). It means that the reactor can use its core for so many days, producing one megawatt of heat energy continuously, for each ton of fuel it contains. Gasoline mileage can be increased by driving very slowly, making few stops, etc. (in short, by making every piston stroke count); but that sort of driving isn't always practical for a delivery truck. In the same way, it is unrealistic to assume that a commercial ship reactor will use its nuclear fuel as efficiently as is theoretically possible. Any fair estimate of nuclear ship costs takes this into account.

Not only must the nuclear ship owner pay for a two- or three-year fuel supply in advance; he also invests in *some* fuel which he knows will *never* be turned into useful energy. Part of its original cost will be refunded eventually, but only when the ship is scrapped and the final reactor core can be sent to the plant which recovers the last of the unused nuclear fuel through elaborate chemical reprocessing.

The owner wants a profit from the extra money he must invest in building the nuclear ship itself. If he spends $10,000,000 extra on construction, he won't be content to save a *total* of only $10,000,000 on fuel during the lifetime of the ship. Either he has borrowed the $10,000,000 (in which case he must gradually replace the money and also pay interest on the loan), or else he has

N.S. Savannah *undergoes a partial refueling. Nuclear fuel always gives relatively good "mileage," but years of cruising must be paid for in advance.*

diverted that amount from some other part of his own business (which could be using it to make money in a different way). A nuke's fuel savings *each year* must be large enough to make up for *a year-by-year share* of the shipowner's entire extra investment cost.

This should also take into account the fact that it may take several years longer to build a nuclear ship and get it licensed than it would take with a conventional ship. The money invested in it sits idle for a long time before profits start rolling in. There are also additional legal and technical fees involved in its licensing.

Eventually, such a nuclear ship will probably have to save *$30,000,000 or more* on fuel in order to be economical. This explains in part why people in the nuclear ship industry have been quoting accurate statistics since the late 1950's which seemed to show that nuclear ships could be money-makers, while people in the shipping industry were really not interested in even trying them until recently.

Shipping companies might spend months or years analyzing comparative figures and their reports might fill many pages; but their conclusions can always be boiled down to a single picture like the one opposite.

Each "money chip" in this drawing represents $1,000,000 a year, and these are very close to the actual figures in one real case. They were computed in 1971 by the Babcock & Wilcox Company for the U.S. Maritime Administration, and they apply to American-built ships of 120,000 shaft horsepower and a specific design. Each vessel could carry more than 2,000 boxcar-sized cargo containers, operating at a speed of 33 knots over a round-trip route of nearly 22,000 miles. The cost figures have been rounded off here to produce a simple drawing, but they are close enough to provide a realistic comparison between nuclear power and fuel oil for one type of merchant ship which is now being constructed. They assume that the ship will be at sea, operating at top speed, about 80 percent of the time, and that the reactor will be quite efficient in using its fuel (producing about 32,000 megawatt-days-per-ton-of-uranium for each core loading). Fuel oil was figured to cost slightly less than $4 a barrel.

All in all, the total cost of building a ship like this and operating it for its entire lifetime under these conditions would be the same whether it used a nuclear reactor or oil-fired boilers. The "voyage costs" are about equal. The basic operating costs are somewhat greater for the nuke

168

ANNUAL COSTS

(Each coin represents one million dollars)

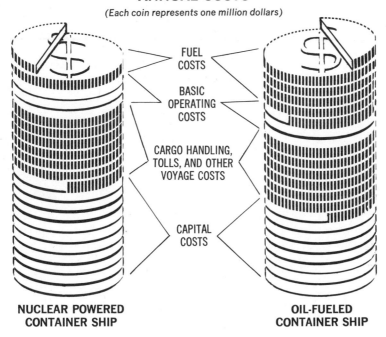

FUEL COSTS	
BASIC OPERATING COSTS	
CARGO HANDLING, TOLLS, AND OTHER VOYAGE COSTS	
CAPITAL COSTS	

NUCLEAR POWERED CONTAINER SHIP

OIL-FUELED CONTAINER SHIP

because of higher salaries and insurance rates, a slightly larger crew, and the need for some special nuclear services. Each year's share of the "capital costs" would be substantially higher for the nuclear version (even if several vessels were built at once, to reduce the construction price of each one); but the annual saving in fuel costs would be so great that things would just balance out overall.

To calculate the "capital cost" annually, the total construction cost ($65,800,000 for the nuke and $46,500,000 for the conventional version) was first divided by twenty. A ship of this kind is expected to stay in service for about twenty years. Then, however, that annual share was roughly tripled. This is necessary to pay the average yearly interest charge on the construction loan and to provide what is considered a fair percentage of return on the money invested by the owners themselves (in this case, about 15 percent per year). This is the major reason why a nuke which costs only $20,000,000 extra to build must save several times that much on fuel during its lifetime in order to pay off.

The annual fuel costs were estimated in much the same way. They are the yearly average for fuel purchases, fuel loading, and reprocessing charges over the whole lifetime of the ship—including an imaginary interest payment for the nuke to make up for the fact that reactor fuel must be bought in such unusual quantities and paid for so far in advance of being used.

In this particular case, the owner of a shipping fleet would probably not pick nuclear power unless he had some special need for it—for example, to operate at top speed on a regular basis. Ordinarily, nuclear power wouldn't increase the ship's income, and it would save nothing in cost. Shipyards are accustomed to building oil-fueled ships, and crews are accustomed to operating them, while nobody has had much experience with nuclear merchantmen. Reactor technology is still changing, and a power plant ordered today might be obsolete before the ship's hull is. Why take a chance?

In many cases, nuclear ships don't show up even this well in an economic analysis. Nevertheless, there are *some* circumstances in which they now show a clear economic advantage. They promise enough extra profit to justify the extra risks; and this is why they are finally attracting serious attention from shipping companies around the world. The reason is that even a slight change in one cost factor or another can now tip the scales—either in favor of the peaceful nukes or in the other direction.

The first big variation is in total fuel cost; this is the most basic. A lot of things affect it, and they are worth discussing individually. Two other variables get less publicity, but businessmen may find them even more critical. One is the interest rate on loans, and the other is government subsidies.

A difference of only a little more than one percent in the interest rate may raise or lower the potential lifetime profits of a nuclear merchant ship by a couple of million dollars. Subsidies are still more important—especially to U.S. firms. These payments by the federal government are intended to encourage this country's shipyards and ship operators, so that the United States can keep up its merchant fleet; and they play such a big role that the industry would simply collapse without them. Most other countries subsidize their merchant navies, too, but they don't all do it in the same way.

Because U.S. wages are so much higher than those in Japan, Germany, Scandinavia, and other shipbuilding centers abroad, Uncle Sam contributes about four dollars out of every ten toward the cost of building big commercial ships here for the merchant fleet. Other subsidies encourage the use of American crews, whose pay is three or four times that of foreign seamen. The exact amount of an operating subsidy depends on complicated calculations, but it has sometimes amounted to more than 70 percent of the crew's wages. Subsidies apply to nuclear as well as nonnuclear ships; yet in several ways they affect the relative profitability of the nukes.

First, the subsidies for ship *construction* are being reduced gradually. The Merchant Marine Act of 1970 provided that the maximum construction subsidies would be cut by two percent each year until July 1, 1975. After that, they should remain steady at 35 percent.

As construction *subsidies* drop, construction *costs* for a shipping company obviously go up. The nuke's normal penalty in building costs is exaggerated. If everything

171

else stays the same, the rise in construction costs makes it tougher for the nuclear version of a ship to show any economic advantage.

Another problem for nuclear ships is that the subsidy rules are written without any specific references to the type of propulsion used, and the experience with them so far is limited to conventional ships. It isn't always clear how these rules should be applied to atomic shipbuilding, but millions of dollars may depend on how they are interpreted. Consider the reactor itself: Is it actually a part of the ship (and thus entitled to one type of subsidy)? Is it *machinery* (perhaps entitling it to a different sort of subsidy)? Or is it fundamentally just a form of *fuel* (which must be bought without any subsidy at all)? Furthermore, construction subsidies are based on the cost difference between building a ship here and having it built in some other country, yet so few peaceful nukes have been built anywhere so far that it's hard to make a fair comparison.

Perhaps the best idea is to have separate subsidy laws which apply exclusively and specifically to nuclear ships, but Congress has found it hard to agree on them. Some legislation to encourage nuclear shipbuilding in the United States has been introduced in every session of Congress since 1959, but the nation will still reach the midpoint of this decade without a single nuclear merchantman. Now that other factors seem favorable, however, it seems likely that a special bill will finally be passed. It will almost certainly authorize two or three ships at once (cutting the construction cost for each through "series production"), and the amount of the government subsidy will probably be spelled out rather precisely.

Subsidies of any type are often criticized as "giveaways," but those in the shipping industry may be a little easier to defend than most. Their backers point out that having a merchant fleet involves more than simple national prestige. During an international emergency, it may be directly involved in national defense. For a country which imports so much petroleum and other vital commodities, it also helps guard against shortages. For a country as deeply involved in world commerce as the United States, it is important in keeping a reasonable trade balance. Nukes help a country's balance-of-payments in an extra way, too—by avoiding fuel purchases overseas. With the United States worried about spending more abroad than foreign nations spend here, nuclear ship advocates point out that by 1990 this country's merchant fleet will cost it more than a billion dollars a year in overseas oil purchases unless it makes a major switch to nuclear power.

Finally, of course, building and operating ships provide jobs for many people whose training and experience are hard to replace if they once fade away. Yet half a dozen nations now have merchant navies which are larger than that of the United States. What can be done? In a world where a number of leading countries seem to be pointing toward commercial atomic fleets before the end of this century, the argument for *nuclear* ship subsidies seems even stronger—at least, if the nukes show economic promise in other ways.

That brings us back to the one basic figure in every cost comparison—the expense of the fuel itself. From now on, if a commercial nuke in any country can't promise a fairly spectacular saving on fuel, it probably won't be built. Furthermore, it probably *shouldn't* be built.

Orders for new ships come in spurts. They slow down temporarily when plenty of ships are available. Then they come in a rush when world trade needs more. In years to come, there is no doubt that many more giant ships will be needed. Nuclear power will actually be *con-sidered* for a relatively small fraction of the ships to be built in the world between now and the year 2000. Comparative costs will probably be studied for only a few thousand vessels; and in most cases the nuclear option will be rejected. In perhaps as many as *several hundred* cases, however, it will win out.

Each individual ship (or at least each group of ships) must be considered separately. In weighing nuclear fuel costs against conventional fuel costs, here are some of the things which will make the difference:

(1) *Power Requirements.* Until a few years ago, all of the largest and most powerful ships in the world were either military vessels or luxury ocean liners. That is changing. The size of individual oil tankers has multiplied nearly twenty times in only twenty years. The largest Japanese supertankers are longer than a nuclear aircraft carrier, and, when fully loaded, each of these giant commercial ships weighs four or five times as much as *Enterprise*. Both the United States and Japan are

Modern supertankers need lots of horsepower. Nuclear propulsion will make economic sense for ships like this during the late 1970's.

building oil tanker fleets of between 250,000 and 500,000 deadweight tons each in order to cut delivery costs. The U.S. Maritime Administration figures that it costs less than half as much to bring oil from the Middle East in one of these monsters as it does in a 50,000-ton tanker.

Because they are relatively slow (15 knots or less), the supertankers still need only a small fraction of the power used by a large passenger liner or warship. Nevertheless, some tankers now have about 40,000 shaft horsepower. This is the lowest power range in which overall nuclear propulsion costs might compete within the next few years.

Ships to carry dry cargo are putting more and more emphasis on speed. The only practical way to increase speed in the long run is by increasing power, so maritime experts are confident that between five hundred and seven hundred and fifty commercial ships of 40,000 shaft horsepower *or more* will be on order in the world's shipyards by 1980. Perhaps one-quarter of them will be at least 80,000 horsepower—like the two nukes already announced by Germany and Japan. Nuclear power would definitely prove to be a profitable investment for some of them.

(2) *Time Spent at Sea.* Ships earn money only by carrying something or somebody from one place to another. To make the greatest profit, they should carry full payloads and stay on the go as much as possible. Shipping companies are constantly looking for (and finding) new ways to do this; and their success means a bonus for nuclear propulsion. The more a nuclear reactor is used, the more money it saves in fuel when compared to conventional power sources.

Container ships are still growing in popularity. When cargo is prepackaged in standard sizes (so that it can be transferred directly from a flatbed rail car to a truck-trailer and then to shipboard), the loading time is reduced from several days to a few hours. Certain ports—such as Bayonne, New Jersey, and Bremerhaven, Germany—now handle almost nothing but containerized cargo. In some harbors, oil-burning ships take less time to unload and load cargo than they do to refuel. Bulk cargoes like coal, ore, and petroleum products are also being handled more rapidly than ever before. Supertankers now load or unload oil in less than a day. This trend makes it easier for nukes to compete.

Completely new kinds of commercial vessels are being developed, too. One basic type is called LASH (*L*ighters *A*board *SH*ips). In this approach, an oceangoing ship is loaded with floatable cargo containers which may be towed ashore or even self-propelled to shore from a point well outside the normal docking area. Such ships would

A single container can serve now as the load for a truck-trailer, flatbed rail car, or a ship. This means quicker loading and shorter stays in port—factors which encourage the use of nuclear ship propulsion.

hardly ever even have to tie up at a wharf. They would save the time normally lost in moving slowly through crowded harbors; and they would spend more days each year traveling at full speed along the open sea-lanes. Some new designs go even further. They should make it possible for the entire engine room and power-plant section of a ship to be separated from that part of the ship's hull which contains cargo. The idea is to turn the propulsion unit into a sort of seagoing locomotive. It would pull into the vicinity of a harbor, unhook its bargelike cargo hull, and pick up another loaded hull for the next leg of its trip. Any schemes like this (which tend to keep the big new ships moving) make nuclear power more appealing economically.

(3) *Cost and Availability of Fuel Oil.* Every time a major petroleum-producing country insists on a rise in prices or mineral royalties, nuclear power seems a bit more attractive. The type of fuel oil used by ships varies considerably in price from port to port, and it goes up and down; but over a period of several years the fuel costs for conventional ships have climbed rather steadily. This has surprised some experts, such as the British Ministry of Trade. In 1971 that agency reported that fuel oil costs were likely to remain the same or even come down, so that there would be "no prospect of nuclear ship propulsion proving commercially competitive in the next two decades." The estimate was obviously wrong.

Some nations' supplies of ship fuel may also be pinched off from time to time by international disputes. Continued troubles in the Middle East are one example. When a shipping company has to look ahead twenty years or so in order to compare its potential earnings from nuclear ships and oil-burning ships, the "profit prophets" must think about such things.

Tankers, of course, may use part of their own cargo as

177

fuel. This is true of the new gas-turbine ships which carry liquefied gas as well as those which carry ordinary oil. But the cost picture for tankers has many special features. First of all, the oil companies themselves are likely to own between one-third and two-thirds of the tankers they use. Such ships rarely need to worry about staying busy, because they are normally guaranteed full cargoes all the time. They don't have the same concern with rapid delivery that some cargo ships do, because petroleum won't spoil. A fleet of oil tankers operates almost like a pipeline; the commodity it carries is part of a continuous flow. It will be used whenever it gets there.

Nevertheless, the people who ship oil from one continent to another also face some growing problems. Larger tankers are more economical, but there are practical limits to their size. They are already too big for some of the world's major shipping canals. The Japanese giant *Nisseki Maru* will scrape bottom in any harbor or channel which isn't at least 89 feet (nearly 30 meters) deep. None of the half dozen largest U.S. tankers which were ordered in 1972 will be able to enter any port along the East Coast or Gulf Coast of the United States. They will need a couple of miles of open sea in which to turn around, and the only efficient way to handle them in this country seems to be by building docks on stilts far offshore (protected by breakwaters), and pumping the cargo in from there. As more oil needs to be transported each year, a logical way seems to be to speed up the tankers themselves. This would make the transocean "pipeline" flow faster, but it would impose even greater demands on the ships' engines. That, in turn, means more shaft horsepower. In time, nuclear-propelled oil tankers seem inevitable.

Stricter environmental laws now promise nuclear ships another advantage. Most large, modern vessels pump aboard seawater ballast as they use up their fuel oil; they must stay low in the water for a fast, smooth, and safe ride. However, many ports now forbid such ships to pump the ballast into the harbor when they refuel. This is to prevent pollution. Ships must either reempty the tanks just before entering coastal waters (a practice which may also be outlawed eventually by international agreement) or else they must make arrangements to pump the useless water into tanks on shore. Either method costs time and money. A nuclear ship has the same displacement during all stages of its voyage, however. This sort of ballasting is unnecessary.

The purpose of this chapter has been to explain why simple comparisons between nuclear ships and conventional ships are so often deceptive and misleading. The special abilities of the nukes may be tremendously important to some commercial shipowners, but almost meaningless to others—a luxury they don't need and can't afford. Furthermore, the fairest comparison in many cases will not be between a single nuke and one oil-burner at all. It may be necessary to match three fast nuclear ships against four or five lower-powered conventional vessels (which could be built for roughly the same cost and could deliver approximately the same total amount of cargo each year while traveling at slower speeds).

Figured that way, the nuclear ships might even save a bit on crew salaries. Building nuclear ships in groups will also help to split up the cost of the special installations nukes need on shore for refueling and overhaul.

Interest rates and subsidies make a big difference. Nuclear power begins to offer a profit on each specific ship-type and route only when power requirements reach a certain level; but a difference of one percent in long-term interest shifts that "break-even point" up or down by about 4,000 shaft horsepower. A rise or fall of ten cents a

There is no question that military subs need large crews to do their job, but peaceful nukes can't afford them.

barrel in the price of fuel oil has just about the same effect.

Passenger liners will probably not be among the first ships to operate profitably with nuclear propulsion. Unless they operated along routes with lots of port stops (which are wasteful for a nuke), they would have trouble finding enough passengers to keep them operating at full capacity on a year-round basis. Furthermore, it's somewhat doubtful that any luxury liner could continue to attract first-class customers for as long as twenty-five years —the time it might take for nuclear power to pay off in fuel savings.

The crews for commercial nukes will surely need special training, and accordingly some of them will probably get extra pay. Crew wages don't make up a very large part of a ship's total cost, however, and the difference won't keep nukes from making a profit unless crews remain unusually large. There should be plenty of merchant marine officers and seamen to operate the peaceful atomic fleets as they appear, if only because of the training and experience provided by nuclear warships. The U.S. Navy has already trained more than 4,000 officers and about 25,000 enlisted men for service on its nukes, and many of these will be available for jobs with commercial shipping firms after ending their terms of military duty.

The use of nuclear ships for peaceful purposes promises to follow the same pattern in which steamships developed. The first steamship to cross the Atlantic Ocean was also named *Savannah*, like the famous nuke which is now retired. The original *Savannah* was also a makeshift vessel; it had sails as well as a steam engine, and it could carry only enough coal to propel it for a small part of its transoceanic journey in 1819. Commercial shippers were skeptical about steam then, and little *Savannah* carried no cargo. Not a single paying passenger signed up for its fancy cabins. The voyage was an economic flop, and so was *Savannah*. Eventually, its steam engine was stripped out. The once-proud ship ended its days as a sailing vessel, hauling cotton between ports along the East Coast. Decades passed before steam engines were used regularly for commercial sea travel, and it took nearly half a century for the big breakthroughs to come. Steam was finally adopted as a result of two other developments: (1) iron hulls, which made possible ships with larger cargo capacity; and (2) improved propulsion systems, using propellers instead of paddle wheels and replacing inefficient engines with ones which needed less coal to produce the same amount of power.

Like steam, nuclear energy will blossom as ships be-

181

come large enough and fast enough to use it effectively. At the same time, the improvements in shipboard nuclear reactors which have resulted from decades of experience with warships and with nuclear plants on shore will find a place in the new peaceful nuclear ships. By the time a few dozen have been built, designs should become more nearly standardized. Then the cost differential between building nuclear and nonnuclear ships will narrow. The special shore facilities needed to service nuclear ships will be developed in most large trading countries—helped in many cases at first by government subsidies.

Steam engines never replaced sails completely. There is still a place for rowboats, too, and for boats and ships with gasoline motors. Nuclear propulsion will never replace conventional steamships totally either, but its role will grow rapidly from now on. And atomic ships *will* make a profit.

CHAPTER NINE

What Comes Next?

Nuclear ships differ from one another, yet as a group they have changed relatively little since the 1950's. More are in service now, of course; and today's reactors are more powerful and efficient than the old ones. But progress in nuclear shipbuilding has been less dramatic than in aviation and rocketry. Considering the rapid pace of technology in general, the time seems ripe for some radical new developments with nuclear ships. A few of these developments are likely to be undertaken during the 1970's, and many will be practical realities before the end of the next decade. Other advances—which can be foreseen today—will take longer.

There is little doubt that nuclear ships of the late 1990's will make current models look like antiques. The changes will fall into three categories: (1) new types of nuclear power sources; (2) new kinds of ships; and (3) new uses for shipboard nuclear power.

First, there will be some attempts to use different types of reactors aboard ships. What kind will they be?

Despite all the publicity about "breeder" reactors (the kind that produce new fissionable fuel material at a slightly faster rate than it takes their original fuel to be used up), breeders do *not* look like an early prospect for ship propulsion. By their very nature, effective breeders aren't very compact. The core must be surrounded by a thick "blanket" of the material which is to be turned into new fuel. Furthermore, it's unlikely that an economical breeder could be built for low power outputs anyway. The *smallest* practical breeder of the type being pushed now by the U.S. Atomic Energy Commission would produce enough energy for a ship with approximately *half a million shaft horsepower*.

By itself, its minimum size might not disqualify the breeder. If ships twice as powerful as *Enterprise* or *United States* are to be built, they can use this much energy and they would have space for the larger power plants. But there are other factors. Fuel represents a larger share of the annual costs for a land-based power plant than it does for a ship; the additional savings from a breeder in the long run would be less significant to a ship operator than they promise to be for electric companies. For a commercial nuclear ship, the unusually large inventory of fuel which must be kept in a breeder constantly would probably be too costly.

In the case of military vessels, the long-term fuel savings make even less difference. Reliability is the chief concern. No new reactor type is going to be installed in a ship until it has been tried out thoroughly on land; and so far only a handful of prototype breeders have been built.

Admiral Rickover has voiced another worry about most breeders—the fact that they would use molten sodium metal to transfer the heat from the core to the steam generators. Remembering his problems with *Seawolf*, Rickover has said flatly that he would never again consider a sodium reactor safe to use on a naval vessel. A metal which can cause an explosion when it touches water is too dangerous to use in large quantities on a

184

ship, he told Congressmen, because the possibility of leaks cannot be ruled out completely.

For many years the admiral has been pressing research and development on what he calls the *"Light Water Breeder Reactor,"* or LWBR. It would use different starting materials, and it would use plain water instead of sodium as its coolant. A demonstration version of the LWBR core is scheduled to be installed in the Shipping-port, Pennsylvania, reactor in 1975, and the force of Admiral Rickover's personality will probably insure that it will be tested on some Navy ship of the future—perhaps an aircraft carrier. Nevertheless, it could be a disappointment. Many reactor experts—inside and out-side the AEC—believe that it won't breed new fuel fast enough to make much difference in cost. Besides, the re-processing of its fuel elements will produce many new problems because of the type of radioactivity involved.

One variety of breeder which *might* fit into the fore-seeable future of nuclear ships is a type which is still largely unknown to the public. It is the *Molten Salt Breeder Reactor*, or MSBR. The fuel in this reactor would be in liquid form—a combination of uranium and plutonium salts which could be kept molten while the reactor was operating. The principle has been proved in reactor experiments at Oak Ridge, Tennessee. MSBR will face its share of problems, too, but it has one advan-tage which could mean a lot to commercial nuclear ship operators: Its fuel can be replaced or replenished easily. Whether this particular technique wins out or not, it's a cinch that the people associated with nuclear merchant ships will concentrate on *some* way to reduce the valu-able time now lost in reactor refueling.

If the advantages of the various breeder reactors for nuclear ships are questionable, however, the potential benefits from *gas-cooled* reactors are not. This is the type of nuclear power source which is most likely to succeed the pressurized-water reactors now being used. Gas-cooled reactors can be designed as breeders, too, but that isn't what makes them promising for ship propulsion.

As Chapter Two explained, water-cooled reactors operate at fairly low temperatures. The steam they generate is far below the temperature-and-pressure combination produced by burning oil inside a conventional ship boiler. Thus nuclear-steam turbines are relatively inefficient; they waste a large amount of a reactor's heat. When a suitable *gas* is used as a reactor's coolant, on the other hand, the operating temperature jumps. Instead of

G.T.S. Admiral William M. Callaghan *(opposite) is a conventionally fueled gas turbine ship. Future generations of ships like this
might use gas-cooled nuclear reactors hooked to the turbines. A
reactor-turbine combination of this type on land (above) was
tested by the U.S. AEC as far back as 1962.*

being limited to about 600° F., it may go to 1400° (the
difference between approximately 315° C. and 760° C.).

Several high-temperature, gas-cooled nuclear reactors
are operating now in various parts of the world. By the
end of the 1970's there will certainly be enough experience with them so that nuclear ship builders might try
them with confidence. When that time comes, however,
power-plant designs will probably take a double step forward. Instead of using a gas-cooled reactor to heat steam
for the usual type of maritime steam turbine, it would
save weight and be much more efficient to hook such a
reactor directly to a *gas* turbine.

Gas-turbine ships are becoming increasingly popular.
They do not all use gas as a *fuel*; the name comes from
the fact that some hot gas (other than ordinary steam) is

187

used to spin the blades of the turbine—which, in turn, spins the ship's propellers. This gas might be heated by an oil fire, or by a reactor.

Gas-turbine ships offer a smooth, quiet ride. They seem especially easy to keep in shape. Their ability to operate without much maintenance will be very important if the reactor coolant is allowed to flow directly through the turbine. This gas would be recirculating constantly, being heated and reheated. Even though a chemically inert gas like helium would probably be used, the turbo machinery would surely pick up some radioactivity after a while. Crewmen couldn't make any extensive repairs at sea. The gas itself could not be allowed to escape either, even though it would have to be kept under high pressure to make sure it transferred heat well. At high pressure, helium leaks right through most metals; and it might be necessary to surround the whole system with prestressed concrete.

The German government group which built the nuclear ship *Otto Hahn* started in 1969 to develop a gas-turbine ship equipped with a gas-cooled reactor, but after about a year of studies they shelved the project. One problem is that if a ship of this kind sank, water might flood the reactor and act like an additional moderator. Nuclear reactions could increase instead of stopping. The Germans decided it would be better to get more experience with gas-cooled reactors and gas turbines in land-based power plants first—before trying to link them at sea. Designing a nuclear-gas-turbine ship safely and economically will not be easy, but the basic idea is good. It will probably be revived before too long.

Aside from reactors, other types of nuclear power sources are mentioned occasionally in connection with nuclear ships; but their practical possibilities are remote. Nuclear fusion is one example. In that process, small

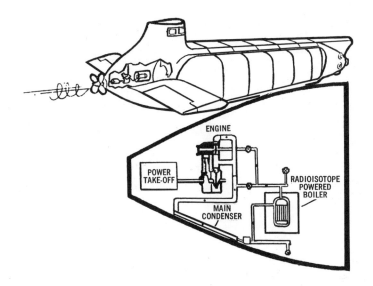

Heat from radioisotopes could propel a sub.

atomic nuclei are fused together—instead of splitting
large nuclei apart. Either fission or fusion releases energy.
The basic fuel for *fusion* (namely, certain forms of hydrogen) exists in seawater; but if fusion reactors are
eventually built they will certainly not be fueled just by
pumping in ocean water—any more than a fission reactor
can be refueled by adding raw uranium ore. Furthermore, fusion reactors will almost certainly have to be
large installations with enormous energy output—not
readily adaptable to propelling anything less than a ship
the size of a city. Finally, fusion is still a long way off. It
isn't clear that practical fusion power plants will be operating *anywhere* before the year 2000.

Power derived from the natural heat of radioisotopes is
at the other end of the size scale from fusion. Heat from
the decay of radioisotopes is the form of nuclear energy
used in the small scientific instrument packages left by
astronauts on the moon. Similar power sources have been
used in the Arctic, the Antarctic, and at the bottom of the

189

sea; but the output of each one is only a few watts. Devices of this type are quite expensive, considering the amount of power they produce. They make sense only in cases and in places where they will be difficult to reach, although they must be counted on to produce energy continuously for a long time.

Radioisotope-fueled generators have been considered as a means of propelling miniature submarines for some military missions. The diagram below shows how this system might work. The submersible illustrated here was never built by the United States, however, and it seems dubious now that it ever will be. Still, it's a possibility.

The *second* way in which nuclear shipbuilding of the future might change is in the design of the ships themselves. Here there are many possibilities. Striking changes may come quickly—within the next few years.

To speed up deliveries by sea, ship designers have begun to experiment again with the ancient idea of twin hulls. The primitive double-canoe, called a catamaran, was both swift and stable. Modern naval architects are applying the shape to broad-decked, oceangoing cargo vessels. Partly because of the difficulty in fitting the concentrated weight of a nuclear reactor into such a vessel, some of the designers suggest that the propulsion unit be built separately. A nuclear "pusher" could be connected to a split cargo hull as shown in the drawings opposite—whisking it through the water at well over 30 knots. The sleek, cargo-laden catamaran would serve as an enormous, high-speed barge. For fast-paced shuttle service like this, nuclear ship propulsion might eventually become economical on relatively short routes (like those across the Atlantic). Each pusher might work with several cargo units so that one catamaran was always being loaded or unloaded at each end of the route while the third was on the high seas. If a sizable fleet of such vessels

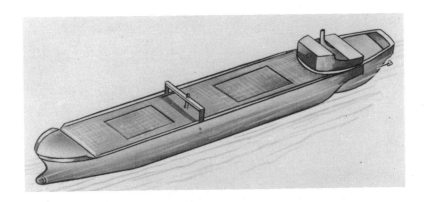

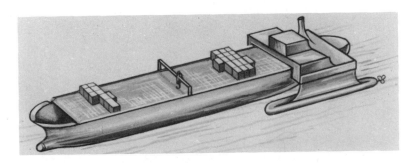

A separable nuclear "pusher" could fit into the rear of a cargo hull (top), or it could straddle the stern (middle). (Below), a "pusher section" fits into the rear of a twin-hulled "catamaran" cargo ship.

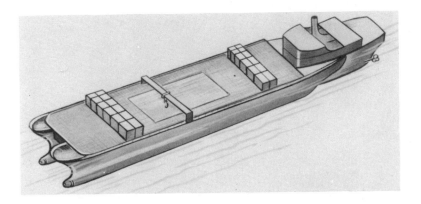

existed, a shipping company would probably alternate crews on the pushers—just as the Navy does now on nuclear patrol subs. The nuclear unit would be in motion almost constantly.

The idea of separate propulsion sections for vessels is not a completely new one, nor is it limited to twin-hulled designs. British coal merchants more than a century ago used a ship called *Connector*, which could split itself into four distinct parts and then be reassembled quickly. One provided power and the other three carried coal—which thus could be delivered promptly to three different docks on a single trip. "Composite ships" have been used in the United States, too, at least since around 1950; one of these is more than 400 feet long (nearly 125 meters). However, those ships are slow, and they travel only between ports along the coast. If the old ideas of the catamaran and the composite ship were blended, the addition of nuclear power would produce an exciting new type of ocean-spanning merchant ship.

A separate propulsion unit need not be a "pusher." It could *pull* cargo sections instead. That's the system used by the long "barge trains" which travel the Mississippi and the great rivers of Europe. Some extend for nearly a quarter of a mile (more than 350 meters). Nuclear tugs have been suggested to lead cargo trains of this type across the ocean, but usually with an extra gimmick. The most common proposal is that the nuclear barge trains travel entirely *underwater*.

One of the first persons to mention this idea was William R. Anderson, the skipper of *Nautilus* on its pioneer voyage to the North Pole. Captain Anderson, who served in Congress after leaving the Navy, is still convinced that a nuclear submarine would be able to tow a string of sausage-shaped, submersible cargo hulls under the ice which covers the Arctic Ocean. The route could

Equipment and crew-space aboard a submarine tanker (above) would cut cargo room (below). But a sub under the Arctic icecap might pull a "train" of petroleum-filled "sausages" behind it.

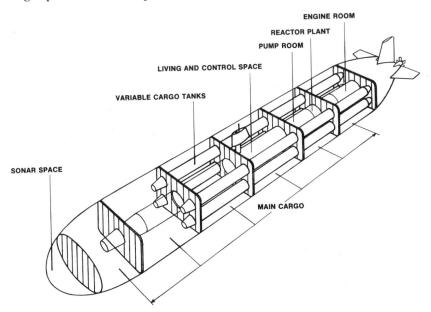

SONAR SPACE

VARIABLE CARGO TANKS

LIVING AND CONTROL SPACE

PUMP ROOM

REACTOR PLANT

ENGINE ROOM

MAIN CARGO

save both time and money in moving cargo from the Atlantic Ocean to the Pacific. It would also make it possible to pick up oil from northern Alaska on a year-round basis.

Snaking through the cavelike darkness under the Arctic ice pack seems like a terrifying prospect for a commercial sea train. Pinnacles of rock reach up from the ocean bottom like stalagmites; pressure ridges of ice plunge down from above like stalactites. Yet bats use their own natural radar to fly safely through caves, and a sub with modern sonar is equally well equipped to speed through the chilly waters safely. Captain Anderson insists that a whole sea train could be moved through, though others who have made the trip fear that the route on the Bering Sea side is too shallow during the winter for regular use.

The first use of a submarine to carry cargo probably occurred during World War I, when Germany did it to boost home-front morale by evading the British blockade. Long after World War II, the United States flirted with the idea of letting subs deliver military equipment during tight battle situations, too. Since the success of *Nautilus*, plans to build nuclear-powered cargo subs have been announced by Japan, Great Britain, Canada, and the United States, but none has gotten past the model-building stage. They *will* appear *eventually*, but probably not before the 1980's.

Comparing cargo subs to surface ships is like comparing nuclear ships to those using fossil fuel. Relative advantages must be weighed against the disadvantages which come with them. There are "break-even points" for speed, size, etc. Above 20 to 25 knots, for instance, submarines can step up their speed with far less power increase than surface ships require. Basically, however,

194

submarines cost more to build; and this difference in construction cost generally tends to increase as their size increases. This is because the whole sub must be enclosed in an expensive, pressure-tight hull.

The nature of a sub hull also suggests something else about cargo submarines; the first ones are more likely to carry liquid than general solid goods. Fluids like oil can be pumped on and off through small openings; hatches big enough to load ordinary crates offer major engineering problems in a hull which *must* be leakproof. Oil could be taken on or discharged by a sub even while it was submerged.

Grain might be loaded and unloaded aboard subs with pneumatic hoses, too, but there isn't likely to be a serious, continuing need for fast, specialized grain-carriers. The

No strangers to the Far North, U.S. nuclear submarines may someday probe beneath the massive Antarctic ice shelves to aid peaceful scientific research.

world supply of petroleum, on the other hand, faces trouble in keeping up with the demand. Even if pipelines are laid across Alaska and Canada, tankers might be called on to bring out some of the products from newly developing oil fields in the Far North. Submarine tankers are bound to be more expensive to operate than surface fleets, but only the subs would be able to reach certain areas during the long Arctic winters. Furthermore, the submarines' speed would insure many more round trips each year—compensating partly for their smaller loads.

In the much more distant future, cargo subs may simply use the Arctic Ocean as a shortcut. The cost of a sub's carrying each ton of goods over a given number of miles will always be high when compared with the cost of surface shipping, yet there *could* be instances when the saving in distance would be great enough to justify it. Heavy trade between Russia's European ports and Japan would be one example. By the time that sort of commerce develops, however, it may be even cheaper to deliver the material in question by air. Except for tankers, nuclear cargo-subs don't look like a very good bet.

When submarine tankers are built, they will probably be far bigger than any other undersea ship ever attempted; but their carrying capacity will still be limited. Double hulls and big ballast tanks take up space. One ambitious design proposed in 1971 by General Dynamics Corporation calls for a sub as long as one of the new surface supertankers, yet it could carry only about *half* as much oil. This is why it seems logical to let such a sub pull a line of "tank cars" behind it. Compared with the propulsion section, these submarine barges would be cheap to construct. They might be rigid, or they might be somewhat flexible (almost like long balloons). They would have to include ballast tanks to adjust depth, but they would need no crew quarters. They would be

Advanced designs for surface or submarine ship hulls (above) are tested at the U.S. Navy's David Taylor Model Basin.

This "Trisec" container ship (below) proposed by Litton combines many new features—gas-turbine engines, a catamaran hull, and water-jet propulsion designed for a speed of 50 knots. Adding a nuclear reactor would be logical in even more advanced designs.

streamlined, and the entire undersea train would be designed to take full advantage of submarine speed.

Some peaceful nukes of the future will have duties other than hauling cargo. There are other tasks in which the endurance of nuclear power systems could be beneficial. One is that of the "fish factory"—the floating processing plant which accompanies fishing fleets.

Commercial fishing is a fairly technical business. Oceanology studies have made it easier to locate and follow the fish crop. As we learn more about the waters of the earth, the fisherman should become still less like a hunter and more like a herdsman—or even a farmer. It will be possible to "manage" life in the sea, encouraging some species to multiply and regulating the harvests. Unlike land crops, however, ocean life is constantly on the move. Nuclear propulsion would be helpful to large factory ships on long missions. Nowadays, such ships do some preliminary processing and provide refrigerated storage. In the future, with plenty of energy available aboard, it might be wise to carry out more of the product preparations at sea. By the time the mother ship of the fleet made one of its infrequent port stops, its cargo could be ready to market. Some seafood (such as shrimp) might even be preserved on board by subjecting it to radiation from the nuclear reactor. Scientists have known for many years that irradiation can eliminate the bacteria which produce decay. In some cases this method is preferable to quick-freezing, because delicate "fresh" flavors are not affected.

Oceanographic research ships will find nuclear power advantageous in the future, too. Long scientific cruises will be made through remote areas like the Arctic, the Antarctic, and the mid-Pacific. Complex scientific instruments will have the convenience of plentiful electricity at sea. There need not be many such ships—perhaps one or two by the end of the century. They will be expensive, but the investment in them will come from governments or groups of governments rather than from private companies. Their long-term "profit" will be in the form of useful new knowledge which couldn't be obtained in any other way.

Some scientific research about the oceans requires working from submarines also. The areas patrolled by missile subs are now quite thoroughly charted, but most of the oceans (which cover most of our planet's surface) are relatively unexplored. Nuclear-powered submersibles are clearly the best all-around tools for the job. Now that the Soviet Union and the United States have agreed to joint space flights, it is only a matter of time before international research groups begin to cooperate in peaceful scientific projects aboard nuclear submarines, too. The first step might be for the United States to allow one of its old nukes to probe the waters under one of the great Antarctic ice shelves. This has not happened so far because the Antarctic Treaty allows any of its signers (including the USSR and several other Communist countries) to inspect equipment used there by any other nation. U.S. Navy officials want the details of their nukes to remain secret.

As a matter of fact, the Russians would probably make no effort to board *Nautilus* or *Seawolf* if it entered the Antarctic. They have argued against on-site inspections anywhere in the world and have declined to exercise this particular right under the Antarctic Treaty. But U.S. willingness to "take the chance" with such an obsolete (yet scientifically valuable) sub might pave the way for more meaningful cooperation in some other scientific sub project.

In time, there is almost sure to be an unclassified version of the Navy's *NR-1*. Perhaps it will be a type that can dive even deeper—possibly a midget nuclear sub with a hull of strong but lightweight fiberglass. It doesn't seem overly optimistic to expect a development like this within ten years or so.

A scientific research sub might use the unusual propeller system conceived some years ago by Commander Frederick Haselton of the Office of Naval Research. The propeller blades project from the hull itself, being mounted on enormous rings which encircle the ship. These rings (two on each sub) would work something like an old-fashioned paddle wheel, except that they would rotate *around* a ship's hull instead of alongside it. The angle of the blades could be varied, so the sub could move forward or back up. It could hover motionless, or it could spin around. This maneuverability would be its greatest asset, and the sub would have to give up speed in return for it. Except for rescue missions, military subs would not consider this a favorable trade. For a research job, a peaceful nuke might welcome it.

Nevertheless, most nuclear vessels will probably continue to be warships. Military nukes too will undergo some changes, and certain new types will appear. First of all, the United States will probably follow the lead of the Soviet Union in arming its subs with "cruise type" missiles—the sort which can change direction in midair. Unlike the old Regulus missiles, however, these will be fired through torpedo tubes or from vertical missile tubes while the sub is still submerged. Navy subs of the future will work closely with surveillance satellites to keep track of potential enemies; and within ten or fifteen years there could be an effort to give a few subs an even better means of scouting an area—namely, their own airplanes.

Military strategists talk more and more these days about making aircraft carriers *smaller*. At the same time, submarines are obviously growing *bigger*. The so-called

V/STOL planes (*V*ertical or *S*hort *T*ake-*Off* and *Land*-ing) don't need much deck space from which to operate, in spite of the fact that they can fly at nearly the speed of sound after they get into the air. It's hard to predict whether the first cross-breed ship will be a small plane carrier with the ability to submerge or an oddly shaped submarine capable of launching a plane or two when it chooses to surface. In either case, however, the plane-toting submersibles will surely be nuclear-propelled ships.

Chiefly for military reasons, *quieter* subs will be developed as time goes on. The turbine-electric-drive sub mentioned in Chapter Four will eliminate noisy reduction gears, but it will still have some vibration from its turbines and other equipment. It will not be completely silent. One way to reduce noise further would be to take out the turbine. That would be difficult but not impossible. Small nuclear power plants have been built (by both the United States and the Russians) which convert heat from a reactor directly into electricity. They aren't very efficient; they waste about nine-tenths of the reactor's heat and energy. Nevertheless, they are as quiet as can be because the generating system contains no moving parts at all. Sooner or later, naval officials will decide to pay the price of using direct-conversion reactors in order to make some subs even harder to detect. Their propellers will still make some noise, and so will the ship's movement through the water. But they will be very, *very* quiet by comparison with other models.

Propellers are due for some design changes, too. In some cases, they will even *disappear* from the nukes of the future. One way of increasing propeller efficiency seems simple; it is to mount twin propellers, one behind the other. The two props would spin on different shafts, but with one shaft fitting inside the other. In this arrangement, if the prop on the inner shaft rotates in a clockwise direction and the one on the outer shaft turns in the opposite direction the ship's power is more effective in pushing the vehicle.

There are unconfirmed reports that the U.S. Navy has mounted such counter-rotating propellers on its nuclear attack submarine *Jack*, hoping to work out the problems of vibration in such a system. Theoretically, this propulsion design could speed up a sub by as much as 50 percent. It will probably produce the fastest subs of all—that is, until the underwater jets take over.

Jetting through the water seems as if it would be easy. Creatures such as the squid and the scallop have been doing it naturally for millions of years. If the water within an object is forced out in one direction, that object moves through the surrounding water in the opposite direction. Jet planes use the same principle as they whiz through the sky, and rockets do the same in outer space.

Small jet-propelled surface boats are a novelty among sportsmen these days. They accelerate rapidly, ride smoothly, and can pass through shallow waters safely because there is neither a rudder nor a propeller extending into the water beneath them. Such a boat is steered by swiveling the direction of the jet. A hydrojet can make sharp turns without much danger of upsetting. Its one drawback is that water-jets are not now as efficient as propellers; a jet boat is often one or two knots slower than an ordinary boat with the same-sized engine.

Nevertheless, underwater jets may some day help nuclear submarines break their next speed barrier. The velocity of propeller-subs depends on certain formulas of basic physics; and there is a speed which they cannot exceed, even in theory. Ramjets follow different formulas, so their top speed is greater—even though they would be extravagant in several ways by reaching it.

A ramjet sub would have to suck in water at its bow, compress it somewhat, and perhaps raise its temperature, then expel it in a powerful stream from its stern. The propulsion equipment to accomplish this would take up a lot of space inside the ship, thus reducing the vessel's ability to carry men and weaponry. An underwater jet would also consume more fuel than a prop-sub while developing the same amount of propulsive power. Its only real advantage would be that one of the speed limits imposed by the laws of hydrodynamics would be lifted. A ramjet sub will be built some day, but only when one of the world's navies decides that its speed is worth the other limitations that go with it.

Speeding up nuclear surface ships will require a different approach. Some engineers believe that nuclear reactors could be installed in oceangoing "air cushion vehicles." These are also called "surface effect ships." They skim across either earth or water at high speed, riding on a thin layer of high-pressure air produced beneath them by fans as they roar along. Such vehicles have a lot of drawbacks, however. They are hard to maneuver, and especially hard to control in a rough sea. The chances are much better that reactors will eventually be used to propel *hydrofoils*.

A hydrofoil is a boat or a ship with wings. The wings are positioned beneath the vessel, so that they pass through water rather than air; but they work very much like an airplane's wings. When enough speed is built up, the water pressure on the underside increases and the pressure along the top of the wing is reduced. This produces "lift"—enough to raise a plane off the ground, or enough to raise a ship's hull completely out of the water. With only the wing (or "foil") and its struts passing through the water, there is less drag. U.S. Navy experiments with small gunboats show that speeds of more than 100 knots can be reached.

Plainview is the largest "flying ship" in the world. By the year 2000, a nuclear-powered ocean liner many times its size may carry tourists across the Atlantic in a single day.

As always, there is a price to pay. The largest hydrofoil built so far weighs a mere 320 tons, but it needs two engines producing the equivalent of nearly 30,000 shaft horsepower to push it along at "only" 50 knots. To double its speed, any hydrofoil must use about five times as much power, so this particular model would need nearly 150,000 shp to travel at 100 knots. No power plant of that capacity would fit into a vehicle of its dimensions, however. With a *conventional* engine of this size, the little ship would have to burn more than its own weight in fuel every day. On the other hand, the shielding around a nuclear reactor would make it too *heavy*. The only way to get a hydrofoil which combines extraordinary speed *and* a reasonable cargo space for more than a short trip seems to be to build a very large one.

Big hydrofoils present big engineering problems. Each

time a hydrofoil's total weight increases, there must be more than a proportional expansion of the wing surface. It's almost like trying to design an elephant that can fly. Some way of matching weight with wing size will probably be found eventually, however, especially in this age when engineering design gets so much help from computers. Yet hydrofoils the size of ocean liners will not get the attention needed to solve the problem until a market for them appears. When that finally happens, they may use either water-jets or advanced-design propellers to push themselves along; but it seems clear that the only basic power source which will be able to give them the tremendous power they demand is the nuclear reactor.

What sort of large ship could ever afford the luxury of expending all this energy to fly through the water at 100 knots? It *could* be a military vessel, but by the year 2000 it might just as easily be a peaceful passenger liner. Who can predict how many tourists might be interested in traveling back and forth between Europe and North America by ship if the ocean voyage were to take only twenty-four hours? Skeptics once insisted that there would never be a demand for the sort of airline service which is now considered essential. Other pessimists were positive that cargo ships would never want to steam faster than about 15 knots. Technically, there is no reason to doubt that a nuclear-powered, jet-propelled, hydrofoil liner could be operating by the end of this century. Realistically, it *may* be.

This book has been devoted to nuclear energy as a means of propelling ships, but there are also other uses for nuclear reactors at sea. For instance, they could be mounted on floating platforms and *towed* from place to place to provide temporary power in times of emergency. The U.S. Army has already tried this with a modified Liberty ship hull rechristened *Sturgis*. According to

Nuclear Ships of the World

Coast Guard regulations and the definition of the international SOLAS agreement, the presence of this or any other sort of reactor on board makes the craft a "nuclear ship." That designation doesn't seem quite right for what is really only a big barge, but the idea of floating power plants may be a good one. Nuclear power plants might also be installed on submerged (or submersible) platforms, which would be occupied by scientists on a more or less permanent basis. Such nuclear-powered installations will probably also be built before the end of this century, but they will not be nuclear ships in the usual sense either. They will have their own separate set of advantages and disadvantages, their own distinct safety considerations, their own unique cost problems.

The purpose of this book—aside from describing the true nuclear ships which have already been built or

Sturgis carries a nuclear power plant to supply electricity to shore bases in emergencies.

designed—has been to show how nuclear energy fits into ship *propulsion* in general. The interrelationships are not all simple. Nuclear propulsion is not a cure-all. Only too often, it is overglamorized, without an adequate explanation of either its handicaps or its real virtues. That treatment is unfair, because it leads to phony optimism, impatience, and possibly discouragement. Nuclear ship propulsion may be a mixed blessing, but it *is* a *blessing*. It deserves better public understanding than it has had, and this book has tried to make a fairer evaluation of it possible.

For the best results, a nuclear reactor can't simply be plopped into a hull which was designed originally for a conventional power source. Ultimately, the greatest progress will be made by fleets of vessels which are conceived from the keel up to get their driving force from the atom. Marine engineers and nuclear engineers must work together. That is the way to reach the full potential of nuclear energy and to minimize its problems. That is the way to expand and improve the nuclear ships of the world.

The Nuclear Lineup

UNITED STATES

Submarines

TYPE: Attack

NAUTILUS (SSN 571)
BUILDER: GD COMMISSIONED: Sept. 30, 1954
PROPULSION: Water-cooled reactor
DISPLACEMENT: 3,500 Tons LENGTH: 320 Feet
The first nuclear submarine. Nautilus was also the world's first true submarine.

TYPE: Attack

Seawolf, second of the nuclear submarines, pioneered in developing new anti-submarine warfare techniques.

SEAWOLF (SSN 575)
BUILDER: GD COMMISSIONED: 1957
PROPULSION: Water-cooled reactor (First used sodium cooled)
DISPLACEMENT: 3,700 Tons LENGTH: 337 Feet

TYPE: Attack

TRITON (SSN 586)
BUILDER: GD COMMISSIONED: 1959
PROPULSION: Two water-cooled reactors
DISPLACEMENT: 5,900 Tons LENGTH: 447 Feet
DECOMMISSIONED: 1969

TYPE: Guided Missile

Halibut was the first nuclear submarine designed to fire Regulus guided missiles. Now a support ship.

HALIBUT (SSGN 587)
BUILDER: MI
COMMISSIONED: 1960
PROPULSION: Water-cooled reactor
DISPLACEMENT: 3,655 Tons LENGTH: 350 Feet

TYPE: Attack

Tullibee was the first nuclear submarine especially designed to detect and destroy enemy submarines below the surface.

TULLIBEE (SSN 597)
BUILDER: GD COMMISSIONED: 1960
PROPULSION: Water-cooled reactor, turbine-electric drive
DISPLACEMENT: 2,300 Tons LENGTH: 273 Feet

TYPE: Attack

NARWHAL (SSN 671)
BUILDER: GD COMMISSIONED: 1969
PROPULSION: Water-cooled reactor
DISPLACEMENT: 4,700 Tons LENGTH: 314 Feet

TYPE: Research & Oceanographic

NR-1
BUILDER: GD DELIVERED: 1969
PROPULSION: Water-cooled reactor
DISPLACEMENT: 400 Tons LENGTH: 140 Feet

TYPE: Attack

GLENARD P. LIPSCOMB (SSN 685)
BUILDER: GD KEEL LAID: 1971
Known as the "quiet submarine," the Glenard P. Lipscomb is equipped with turbine-electric drive in place of the conventional steam turbine.

TYPE: Fleet Ballistic Missile
First nuclear submarine designed to fire the Polaris intermediate range ballistic missile from submerged or surfaced positions.

GEORGE WASHINGTON (SSBN 598)
BUILDER: GD COMMISSIONED: 1959
PROPULSION: Water-cooled reactor
DISPLACEMENT: 6,000 Tons LENGTH: 380 Feet

PATRICK HENRY (SSBN 599)
BUILDER: GD COMMISSIONED: 1960

THEODORE ROOSEVELT (SSBN 600)
BUILDER: MI COMMISSIONED: 1961

ROBERT E. LEE (SSBN 601)
BUILDER: NNS&D COMMISSIONED: 1960

ABRAHAM LINCOLN (SSBN 602)
BUILDER: PNS COMMISSIONED: 1961

TYPE: Fleet Ballistic Missile
Lead ship of a second generation of Polaris submarines, this is the first submarine designed from the keel up for this mission.

ETHAN ALLEN (SSBN 608)
BUILDER: GD COMMISSIONED: 1961
PROPULSION: Water-cooled reactor
DISPLACEMENT: 6,900 Tons LENGTH: 410 Feet

SAM HOUSTON (SSBN 609)
BUILDER: NNS&D COMMISSIONED: 1962

THOMAS A. EDISON (SSBN 610)
BUILDER: GD COMMISSIONED: 1962

JOHN MARSHALL (SSBN 611)
BUILDER: NNS&D COMMISSIONED: 1962

THOMAS JEFFERSON (SSBN 618)
BUILDER: NNS&D COMMISSIONED: 1963

Lafayette began a third generation of Polaris submarines and embodies more sophisticated systems than predecessors. Now being converted to fire the Poseidon missile.

TYPE: Fleet Ballistic Missile

LAFAYETTE (SSBN 616)
BUILDER: GD COMMISSIONED: 1963
PROPULSION: Water-cooled reactor
DISPLACEMENT: 7,300 Tons LENGTH: 425 Feet

ALEXANDER HAMILTON (SSBN 617)
BUILDER: GD COMMISSIONED: 1963

ANDREW JACKSON (SSBN 619)
BUILDER: MI COMMISSIONED: 1963

JOHN ADAMS (SSBN 620)
BUILDER: PNS COMMISSIONED: 1964

JAMES MONROE (SSBN 622)
BUILDER: NNS&D COMMISSIONED: 1963

NATHAN HALE (SSBN 623)
BUILDER: GD COMMISSIONED: 1963

WOODROW WILSON (SSBN 624)
BUILDER: MI COMMISSIONED: 1963

HENRY CLAY (SSBN 625)
BUILDER: NNS&D COMMISSIONED: 1964

DANIEL WEBSTER (SSBN 626)
BUILDER: GD COMMISSIONED: 1964

JAMES MADISON (SSBN 627)
BUILDER: NNS&D COMMISSIONED: 1964

TECUMSEH (SSBN 628)
BUILDER: GD COMMISSIONED: 1964

DANIEL BOONE (SSBN 629)
BUILDER: MI COMMISSIONED: 1964

JOHN C. CALHOUN (SSBN 630)
BUILDER: NNS&D COMMISSIONED: 1964

ULYSSES S. GRANT (SSBN 631)
BUILDER: GD COMMISSIONED: 1964

VON STEUBEN (SSBN 632)
BUILDER: NNS&D COMMISSIONED: 1964

CASIMIR PULASKI (SSBN 633)
BUILDER: GD COMMISSIONED: 1964

STONEWALL JACKSON (SSBN 634)
BUILDER: MI COMMISSIONED: 1964

SAM RAYBURN (SSBN 635)
BUILDER: NNS&D COMMISSIONED: 1964

NATHANAEL GREENE (SSBN 636)
BUILDER: PNS COMMISSIONED: 1964

BENJAMIN FRANKLIN (SSBN 640)
BUILDER: GD COMMISSIONED: 1965

SIMON BOLIVAR (SSBN 641)
BUILDER: NNS&D COMMISSIONED: 1965

KAMEHAMEHA (SSBN 642)
BUILDER: MI COMMISSIONED: 1965

GEORGE BANCROFT (SSBN 643)
BUILDER: GD COMMISSIONED: 1966

LEWIS & CLARK (SSBN 644)
BUILDER: NNS&D COMMISSIONED: 1965

JAMES K. POLK (SSBN 645)
BUILDER: GD COMMISSIONED: 1966

GEORGE C. MARSHALL (SSBN 654)
BUILDER: NNS&D COMMISSIONED: 1966

HENRY L. STIMSON (SSBN 655)
BUILDER: GD COMMISSIONED: 1966

GEORGE WASHINGTON CARVER (SSBN 656)
BUILDER: NNS&D COMMISSIONED: 1966

FRANCIS SCOTT KEY (SSBN 657)
BUILDER: GD COMMISSIONED: 1966

MARIANO G. VALLEJO (SSBN 658)
BUILDER: MI COMMISSIONED: 1966

WILL ROGERS (SSBN 659)
BUILDER: GD COMMISSIONED: 1967

TYPE: Attack
First production model submarine. Skate opened up the Arctic as a year-round operation area for submarines.

SKATE (SSN 578)
BUILDER: GD COMMISSIONED: 1957
PROPULSION: Water-cooled reactor
DISPLACEMENT: 2,500 Tons LENGTH: 268 Feet

SWORDFISH (SSN 579)
BUILDER: PNS COMMISSIONED: 1958

SARGO (SSN 583)
BUILDER: MI COMMISSIONED: 1958

SEADRAGON (SSN 584)
BUILDER: PNS COMMISSIONED: 1959

TYPE: Attack
A whale-shaped hull coupled with nuclear power made this class the world's fastest and most maneuverable submarine.

SKIPJACK (SSN 585)
BUILDER: GD COMMISSIONED: 1959
PROPULSION: Water-cooled reactor
DISPLACEMENT: 3,000 Tons LENGTH: 252 Feet

SCAMP (SSN 588)
BUILDER: MI COMMISSIONED: 1961

SCORPION (SSN 589)
BUILDER: GD COMMISSIONED: 1960
Lost in the Atlantic 5/21/68

SCULPIN (SSN 590)
BUILDER: ING COMMISSIONED: 1961

SHARK (SSN 591)
BUILDER: NNS&D COMMISSIONED: 1961

SNOOK (SSN 592)
BUILDER: ING COMMISSIONED: 1961

TYPE: Attack

This attack class is an advance of the Skipjack design. Somewhat larger and heavier, it is one of the Navy's prime anti-submarine warfare weapons.

PERMIT (SSN 594)
BUILDER: MI COMMISSIONED: 1962
PROPULSION: Water-cooled reactor
DISPLACEMENT: 3,750 Tons LENGTH: 279 Feet

PLUNGER (SSN 595)
BUILDER: MI COMMISSIONED: 1962

BARB (SSN 596)
BUILDER: ING COMMISSIONED: 1963

POLLACK (SSN 603)
BUILDER: NYS COMMISSIONED: 1964

HADDO (SSN 604)
BUILDER: NYS COMMISSIONED: 1964

JACK (SSN 605)
BUILDER: PNS COMMISSIONED: 1967

TINOSA (SSN 606)
BUILDER: PNS COMMISSIONED: 1964

DACE (SSN 607)
BUILDER: ING COMMISSIONED: 1964

GUARDFISH (SSN 612)
BUILDER: NYS COMMISSIONED: 1966

FLASHER (SSN 613)
BUILDER: GD COMMISSIONED: 1966

GREENLING (SSN 614)
BUILDER: GD COMMISSIONED: 1967

GATO (SSN 615)
BUILDER: GD COMMISSIONED: 1968

HADDOCK (SSN 621)
BUILDER: ING COMMISSIONED: 1967

THRESHER (SSN 593)
BUILDER: PNS COMMISSIONED: 1961
Lost in the Atlantic 4/10/63

TYPE: Attack

An advance over the Permit design, this is the Navy's largest class of nuclear submarines.

STURGEON (SSN 637)
BUILDER: GD COMMISSIONED: 1967
PROPULSION: Water-cooled reactor
DISPLACEMENT: 4,200 Tons LENGTH: 292 Feet

WHALE (SSN 638)
BUILDER: GD(Q) COMMISSIONED: 1968

TAUTOG (SSN 639)
BUILDER: ING COMMISSIONED: 1968

GRAYLING (SSN 646)
BUILDER: PNS COMMISSIONED: 1969

POGY (SSN 647)
BUILDER: NYS/ING COMMISSIONED: 1971

ASPRO (SSN 648)
BUILDER: ING COMMISSIONED: 1969

SUNFISH (SSN 649)
BUILDER: GD(Q) COMMISSIONED: 1969

PARGO (SSN 650)
BUILDER: GD COMMISSIONED: 1968

QUEENFISH (SSN 651)
BUILDER: NNS&D COMMISSIONED: 1966

PUFFER (SSN 652)
BUILDER: ING COMMISSIONED: 1969

RAY (SSN 653)
BUILDER: NNS&D COMMISSIONED: 1967

SAND LANCE (SSN 660)
BUILDER: PNS COMMISSIONED: 1971

LAPON (SSN 661)
BUILDER: NNS&D COMMISSIONED: 1967

GURNARD (SSN 662)
BUILDER: MI COMMISSIONED: 1968

HAMMERHEAD (SSN 663)
BUILDER: NNS&D COMMISSIONED: 1968

SEA DEVIL (SSN 664)
BUILDER: NNS&D COMMISSIONED: 1969

GUITARRO (SSN 665)
BUILDER: MI COMMISSIONED: 1972

HAWKBILL (SSN 666)
BUILDER: MI COMMISSIONED: 1971

BERGALL (SSN 667)
BUILDER: GD COMMISSIONED: 1969

SPADEFISH (SSN 668)
BUILDER: NNS&D COMMISSIONED: 1969

SEAHORSE (SSN 669)
BUILDER: GD COMMISSIONED: 1969

FINBACK (SSN 670)
BUILDER: NNS&D COMMISSIONED: 1970

PINTADO (SSN 672)
BUILDER: MI COMMISSIONED: 1971

FLYING FISH (SSN 673)
BUILDER: GD COMMISSIONED: 1970

TREPANG (SSN 674)
BUILDER: GD COMMISSIONED: 1970

BLUEFISH (SSN 675)
BUILDER: GD COMMISSIONED: 1971

BILLFISH (SSN 676)
BUILDER: GD COMMISSIONED: 1971

DRUM (SSN 677)
BUILDER: MI COMMISSIONED: 1972

ARCHERFISH (SSN 678)
BUILDER: GD COMMISSIONED: 1971

SILVERSIDES (SSN 679)
BUILDER: GD COMMISSIONED: 1972

WILLIAM H. BATES (SSN 680)
BUILDER: ING COMMISSIONED:

BATFISH (SSN 681)
BUILDER: GD COMMISSIONED: 1972

TUNNY (SSN 682)
BUILDER: ING COMMISSIONED:

PARCHE (SSN 683)
BUILDER: ING COMMISSIONED:

CAVALLA (SSN 684)
BUILDER: GD COMMISSIONED: 1973

L. MENDEL RIVERS (SSN 686)
BUILDER: NNS&D COMMISSIONED:

RICHARD B. RUSSELL (SSN 687)
BUILDER: NNS&D COMMISSIONED:

TYPE: Attack

Known as the "high-speed submarine," the SSN 688 class represents an advance in length and weight over the Sturgeon design. Under construction.

LOS ANGELES (SSN 688)
BUILDER: NNS&D KEEL LAID: 1972
PROPULSION: Water-cooled reactor
DISPLACEMENT: 6,800 Tons LENGTH: 360 Feet

BATON ROUGE (SSN 689)
BUILDER: NNS&D COMMISSIONED:

PHILADELPHIA (SSN 690)
BUILDER: GD COMMISSIONED:

(SSN 691)
BUILDER: NNS&D COMMISSIONED:

OMAHA (SSN 692)
BUILDER: GD COMMISSIONED:

(SSN 693)
BUILDER: NNS&D COMMISSIONED:

(SSN 694)
BUILDER: GD COMMISSIONED:

(SSN 695)
BUILDER: NNS&D COMMISSIONED:

(SSN 696)
BUILDER: GD COMMISSIONED:

(SSN 697)
BUILDER: GD COMMISSIONED:

(SSN 698)
BUILDER: GD COMMISSIONED:

(SSN 699)
BUILDER: GD COMMISSIONED:

ABBREVIATIONS

GD	Electric Boat Division of General Dynamics, Groton, Conn.
GD(Q)	Quincy Shipbuilding Division of General Dynamics, Quincy, Mass.
ING	Ingalls Nuclear Shipbuilding Division of Litton Industries, Pascagoula, Miss.
MI	Mare Island Naval Shipyard, Vallejo, Calif.
NNS&D	Newport News Shipbuilding & Drydock Co., Newport News, Va.
NYS	New York Shipbuilding Corporation, Camden, N.J.
PNS	Portsmouth Naval Shipyard, Portsmouth, N.H.
BETH	Bethlehem Shipyard, Quincy, Mass.

Surface Ships

AIRCRAFT CARRIERS

ENTERPRISE (CVAN 65)
BUILDER: NNS&D COMMISSIONED: 1961
PROPULSION: Eight water-cooled reactors
DISPLACEMENT: 89,400 Tons
LENGTH: 1,101 Feet
Her 280,000 shaft horsepower made the first nuclear carrier the most powerful ship in history.

NIMITZ (CVAN 68)
BUILDER: NNS&D LAUNCHED: 1972
PROPULSION: Two water-cooled reactors, equivalent to Enterprise's eight
DISPLACEMENT: 95,000 Tons
LENGTH: 1,092 Feet
Expected to cruise for 13 years before refueling is required.

EISENHOWER (CVAN 69)
BUILDER: NNS&D KEEL LAID: 1970
Delivery expected in 1975

NEW MULTIMISSION CARRIER (CVN 70)
The next nuclear carrier planned will not be either a CVA type (designed primarily to launch surface attacks) or a CVS type (aimed principally at antisubmarine warfare). It will be intended to handle either or both missions, so it will be designated CV (plus N for nuclear).

GUIDED MISSILE FRIGATES

BAINBRIDGE (DLGN 25)
BUILDER: BETH COMMISSIONED: 1962
PROPULSION: Two water-cooled reactors
DISPLACEMENT: 8,430 Tons LENGTH: 564 Feet

TRUXTUN (DLGN 35)
BUILDER: NYS COMMISSIONED: 1967
DISPLACEMENT: 9,000 Tons LENGTH: 564 Feet

CALIFORNIA (DLGN 36)
BUILDER: NNS&D LAUNCHED: 1971
PROPULSION: Two water-cooled reactors capable of 10 years' normal ship operation before refueling
DISPLACEMENT: 10,000 Tons LENGTH: 596 Feet

SOUTH CAROLINA (DLGN 37)
BUILDER: NNS&D LAUNCHED: 1972
DISPLACEMENT: 10,000 Tons LENGTH: 596 Feet

VIRGINIA (DLGN 38)
Scheduled for service by 1975, this is the first of about five new guided missile frigates intended to join nuclear carriers in atomic task forces.

GUIDED MISSILE CRUISER

LONG BEACH (CGN 9)
BUILDER: BETH   COMMISSIONED: 1961
PROPULSION: Two water-cooled reactors
DISPLACEMENT: 17,350 Tons   LENGTH: 721 Feet

MERCHANT SHIP

N.S. SAVANNAH
BUILDER: NYS   NUCLEAR PLANT: The Babcock
& Wilcox Co.
KEEL LAID: 1958   LAUNCHED: 1959
ENTERED OPERATION: 1961
DISPLACEMENT: 22,000 Tons
LENGTH: 595.5 Feet
MAXIMUM POWER: 22,000 shp
Out of service; survives as a floating museum
for the city of Savannah.

SOVIET UNION

Submarines

NOVEMBER (N) CLASS
The first Russian nuclear sub was a production
model of this series. About 15 were built, and
at least one has been lost at sea.
DISPLACEMENT: About 3,500 Tons
LENGTH: About 330 Feet

ECHO (E) CLASS
Longer and much heavier than the "N," this
class carries air-breathing cruise missiles with
at least 400 mile range. More than two dozen
are in service.

HOTEL (H) CLASS
Easily recognized by the very bulky superstructure, which houses three upright ballistic
missiles of an early design. Nearly a dozen
subs of this class were built.

YANKEE (Y) and DELTA (D) CLASSES
Similar to, but somewhat larger than U.S. FBM
subs. Each Y-type carries 16 Polaris-type ballistic missiles; a Delta is modified to hold 12
of a newer kind corresponding to Poseidon.
More than 40 are in service or being built.

CHARLIE (C) CLASS

Trimmer and faster than the Echo class, this type carries eight cruise missiles of greater range. Began to enter service in late 1960's.

VICTOR (V) CLASS

High-speed attack submarine was successor to "N" class as a basic killer sub for the USSR.

PAPA (P) CLASS

Carries cruise missiles, presumably for use against surface ships. Has some advantages over "C" type.

Icebreakers

LENIN

BUILDER: Kirov Elektrosia Works, Leningrad
LAUNCHED: 1957 ENTERED SERVICE: 1959
OUT OF SERVICE: 1966-69
PROPULSION: Electric drive, with power supplied by two water-cooled reactors producing up to 44,000 shp
DISPLACEMENT: 16,000 Tons LENGTH: 440 Feet

ARKTIKA

Planned since 1964, but service date still uncertain. Longer than Lenin, displacing about 25,000 tons.

UNITED KINGDOM

BALLISTIC MISSILE FIRING SUBMARINES

(Each is 425 feet long and displaces about 8,400 tons submerged)

RESOLUTION (S 22)
BUILDER: VICKERS COMMISSIONED: 1967

REPULSE (S 23)
BUILDER: VICKERS COMMISSIONED: 1968

RENOWN (S 26)
BUILDER: CL COMMISSIONED: 1969

REVENGE (S 27)
BUILDER: CL COMMISSIONED: 1969

ATTACK SUBMARINE

DREADNOUGHT (S 101)
BUILDER: VICKERS COMMISSIONED: 1963
DISPLACEMENT: 4,000 tons submerged
LENGTH: 265 Feet
Prototype for the British Nuclear navy.

FLEET SUBMARINES

(Each is 17 feet longer and about 500 tons heavier than Dreadnought)

VALIANT (S 102)
BUILDER: VICKERS COMMISSIONED: 1966

WARSPITE (S 103)
BUILDER: VICKERS COMMISSIONED: 1967

CHURCHILL (S 104)
BUILDER: VICKERS COMMISSIONED: 1970

CONQUEROR (S 105)
BUILDER: CL COMMISSIONED: 1971

COURAGEOUS (S 106)
BUILDER: VICKERS COMMISSIONED: 1971

SWIFTSURE (S 107)
BUILDER: VICKERS KEEL LAID: 1969

SOVEREIGN (S 108)
BUILDER: VICKERS

SUPERB (S 109)
BUILDER: VICKERS Ordered in 1970

(S 110)
BUILDER: VICKERS Ordered in 1971

(S 111)
BUILDER: VICKERS Ordered in 1972

ABBREVIATIONS

VICKERS Vickers Ltd. Shipbuilding Group, Barrow.
CL Cammell Laird & Co., Ltd., Birkenhead.

FRANCE

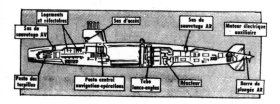

Ballistic Missile Firing Submarines

(Each is 420 feet long and displaces 8,000 tons at the surface)

REDOUBTABLE
Began patrols in 1972

TERRIBLE
Operational since 1972

FOUDROYANT
Launched in 1971

INDOMPTABLE
Scheduled to be
operational 1976

FEDERAL REPUBLIC OF GERMANY

OTTO HAHN (ore carrier)

BUILDER: Kieler Howaldtswerke

NUCLEAR PLANT: Babcock/Interatom

OWNER-OPERATOR: Gesellschaft für Kernenergieverwertung in Schiffbau und Schiffahrt, mbH. (Company for the Utilization of Nuclear Energy in Shipbuilding and Shipping, Ltd.), Hamburg.

PROPULSION: Water-cooled reactor, delivering up to 11,000 shp

DISPLACEMENT: 25,812 Tons

LENGTH: 564.3 Feet
Operational since 1968. Refueled in 1972.

JAPAN

MUTSU (specialized cargo ship)

SHIPBUILDER: Ishikawajima-Harima Heavy Industries Co., Ltd. (Tokyo).

REACTOR MANUFACTURER: Mitsubishi Atomic Power Industries, Inc.

PROPULSION: Water-cooled reactor, designed to produce 10,000 shp

DISPLACEMENT: 10,400 Tons

LENGTH: 428.2 Feet
Operational since 1973

German-Japanese Joint Venture

In 1971 the two governments agreed to cooperate in building two nuclear-powered container ships of about 80,000 shaft horsepower each. Japan accepted the responsibility for the ship hulls and Germany is to handle the nuclear power plants, as soon as agreement can be reached with commercial operators.

Index

218

Index

About the Author

JOSEPH M. DUKERT has been associated with nuclear energy projects since the late 1950's, and his first "science for the layman" book—*Atompower*—was published in 1962. An award-winning film producer, he is now a communications consultant to industry and government. His research for this book included visits to several types of nuclear ships and discussions with experts from a number of countries.

Mr. Dukert writes for the U.S. Atomic Energy Commission's World of the Atom series, and he has also been a consultant to the U.S. Department of Commerce and the U.S. Information Agency. His articles have appeared in a variety of leading magazines. He is married to the former Betty Cole, associate producer of NBC's *Meet the Press*, and they live in a suburb of Washington, D.C.